LIVE AND WORK IN
BRAZIL

Visit our How To website at **www.howto.co.uk**

At **www.howto.co.uk** you can engage in conversation with some of our authors – all of whom have 'been there and done that' in their specialist fields. You can get access to special offers and additional content but, most importantly, you will be able to engage with, and become a part of, a wide and growing community of people just like yourself.

At **www.howto.co.uk** you'll be able to talk to, and share tips with, people who have similar interests and are facing similar challenges in their lives. People who, just like you, have the desire to change their lives for the better – be it through moving to a new country, starting a new business, growing their own vegetables, or writing a novel.

At **www.howto.co.uk** you'll find the support and encouragement you need to help make your aspirations a reality.

How To Books strives to present authentic, inspiring, practical information in their books. Now, when you buy a title from **How To Books**, you get even more than words on a page.

LIVE AND WORK IN
BRAZIL

All you need to know about life, work and property
in one of the world's fastest-growing economies

ROMASA STOREY

howtobooks

How To Books Ltd
Spring Hill House, Spring Hill Road
Begbroke, Oxford OX5 1RX, United Kingdom
Tel: 01865 375794 Fax: 01865 379162
info@howtobooks.co.uk
www.howtobooks.co.uk

British Library Cataloguing in Publication Data
A catalogue record for this book is available from
the British Library.

First published 2009

ISBN: 978 1 84528 310 0

Cover design by Baseline Arts Ltd, Oxford
Typeset by *specialist* publishing services ltd, Montgomery
Produced for How To Books by Deer Park Productions, Tavistock

Photos in Photo Gallery and page 31 reproduced by kind permission of EMBRATUR's Image Database
at www.braziltour.com/brazilnetwork. Photos on all other pages from iStock.com.

Printed and bound by Bell & Bain Ltd, Glasgow

Contents

Preface

Many British people living a fairly normal life in the UK were being urged to buy 'a place in the sun' by the programme makers of the same name. Although the places offered seemed to live up to the name of the programme, they were usually not 'adventurous' places in the sun.

Returning from a holiday in the Maldives and Sri Lanka, we were tempted by Sri Lanka and nearly bought a house in Galle at the southern tip. However, the government there had decided to impose a 100% property tax on foreigners buying land so we did not proceed. This was just as well because a couple of months later, Galle (and probably the house which we had nearly bought) were hit by the tsunami.

An alternative adventurous playground somewhere off the well-trodden 'Caribbean' track was Central America. We were offered an island just off the Nicaraguan coast. The idyllic tropical paradise, which was going for a song, turned out to be a battleground for armed encounters between the owners of the paper title and the local population, who claimed customary rights over the land.

Drawing for breath, we stopped searching and, instead we decided to content ourselves with buying an old Rolls Royce; we spent a small fortune on going to see one in North Wales and having it tested. We reckoned that it was over-priced and returned home. Then we found the website of a car broker who deals, nearly exclusively, in Rolls Royce and Bentley motor cars. We almost went to view a magnificent two door RR Silver Cloud III with 'Chinese eye' headlamps. However, before we got that far, the broker telephoned us and said that he had to be quick because he was telephoning us on his mobile telephone from Brazil. Brazil! Suddenly, the penny dropped. *This* might be an adventurous place to live.

Some research suggested that Brazil is what the rather arrogant 'western world' calls an 'emerging economy'. Famously rich in natural resources (now even oil has been found there), vast and beautiful, it merited our further consideration.

This book is the result of our direct experience of coming to explore and to live in Brazil. It has not been an easy process, not least because it is a country with certain confusions and contradictions and mixtures of irreconcilable differences (such as the practice of voodoo and the acceptance of petty pilfering).

The aim of this book is to make moving to Brazil easier for others than it has been for us. We aim to assist those who wish to move to Brazil permanently or for just a part of the year. However, even moving house in the same town or city is stressful enough – without moving countries and continents, 7,000 miles from all that is familiar. Therefore, it would be foolish to claim that this (or any book) can make the process of *full* emigration completely stress-free, but we'll try our best to make it as painless as possible.

Chapter 1

Introduction

Brazil is a massive country with lots going for it: a rich history, colourful culture and stunning scenery. What a place . . .

HISTORY

Brazil is the fifth largest country in the world, after (in order) Russia, Canada, China and the USA. It has a land area of 8.5 million square kilometres and a population of 188 million people. It was 'discovered' by Portuguese explorers, headed by Pedro Alvares Cabral in 1500. Before this its population comprised Amerindians. It was gradually colonized by the Portuguese and exploited originally for its hardwoods and later for sugar cane and coffee. Mining for gold and precious stones, including diamonds was important. Precious stones are still mined in the state of Minais Gerais (meaning 'general mines'), especially emerald, aquamarine, topaz (including precious imperial topaz) and tourmaline.

The country's wealth was built on the enslavement of the indigenous population and, later, of Africans. Slavery was officially abolished (late) in 1888, as a result of a law called the Golden Law of Princess Isabel, of whom there is a statue (presumably in gratitude) just opposite the former Meridian Hotel (now the Iberostar) in Copacabana, Rio de Janeiro. This law was enforced with help from the British Navy which blockaded the ports, particularly in the North East where, as Peter Robb tells us in A Death in Brazil, the importation of slaves clandestinely continued for a while; the 'imports' being called 'chickens'.

At first Brazil was simply a colony of the Portuguese. The official language is Brazilian Portuguese, which differs from European Portuguese much as American English differs from the Queen's English. There are language courses and CDs that offer an opportunity to learn each version of the language. Minority languages are spoken as a first language amongst some small residual pockets of the original population. These include Tupi, Guarani, Kaingang, Caraja, Caribe, Tucano, Arara, Terena, Bororo, Apalai, Canela, and Nadeb. There is also German (spoken by 1.5m), Italian (spoken by 0.5m), Japanese (spoken by 0.4m) and Korean (spoken by 37,000).

After the Brazilian empire of the Portuguese, there was an independent Brazilian empire, but still under a member of the ruling Portuguese royal family, the House of Braganza. On 15th November 1881, a military coup imposed a federal republic. Because of its great natural riches, many immigrants from Europe, the Middle East, Japan and Asia swelled a population that had already become genetically mixed by interbreeding, between the indigenous population, the Portuguese and Africans.

RELIGIONS

As well as their language, the Portuguese brought with them their religion: Roman Catholicism. Brazil is said to have the largest Roman Catholic population of any country. However, there is a twist on this because there is a growing evangelical Christian church movement, which is attracting numbers of people who are, anyway, often caught between the strict doctrines of the Roman Catholic Church and their own inclinations. Many Brazilians are also caught up in the voodoo practices of their African ancestors.

CHARACTER

The Brazilian personality is difficult for 'westerners' to fathom. The people seem friendly and happy – and they are, but this is not the end of the story because they also seem to see things only from one, restricted point of view. If you happen to be bamboozled into a hard bargain by a mixture of desperate importunity, sob-story and vast over-valuation of the goods on offer (which may or may not be genuine, in any event), don't say that you have not been warned. In a similar vein, do not buy jewellery or precious or semi-precious stones from a man with a box or a stall in the street.

If you have travelled in some parts of Asia you might well have encountered one type of 'con' trick phenomenon already – a helpful 'driver' appearing at the hotel steps, asking only that you pay his petrol, with an offer of visiting gem 'museums' – where, lo and behold the exhibits are for sale! Sales are pressed, at prices set according to your nationality; where you are staying; what you are wearing; where you have been eating and any obvious give-aways like precious stones already on fingers: presumably the actual market value of the item figures somewhere in the calculation but, often, it is difficult to discern where.

Another thing to watch out for is being 'introduced' to shops and tradesmen by people helpfully masquerading as good Samaritans who 'just want to be your friend'. In fact what they are up to is delivering a Gringo, in return for a kickback commission – which will be written into the cost of the goods or services that you purchase (which may well, in any event, be overpriced). The amount of this commission will be at least the amount of discount (*a vista*) allowed for cash payments (as opposed to instalment payments) which would normally be given to the money lender.

It is necessary to watch your possessions and yourselves in Brazil. In big cities, the threat of violence is notoriously omnipresent, but if you go about carefully, it can usually be avoided.

It is plainly bad form for immigrants to criticise a host country or its people (after all, if you don't like them, leave!). The purpose of these warnings here in this book is not to criticise, nor to urge reform, but just to advise and warn newcomers against common forms of naked exploitation.

Moreover, if you get into a scrape or dispute with a Brazilian, it will be a most extraordinary Brazilian who will not, as a matter of course, be inclined to support his countryman; although such people, especially amongst the more educated and those who have travelled outside Brazil, do exist.

There is not so much racial discrimination here – not least because there is such a mixture of races within the Brazilian people – but there is an open bias against *gringos* – except when striking deals. There's also, a scarcely concealed resentment of foreigners shown by some people.

GEOGRAPHY AND CLIMATE

Brazil is easily the biggest country in South America and borders all of the others, except Chile and Ecuador. It stretches from the equator to just over 30° south (at its longest point, 2,731 miles) and (at its widest point, 2,684 miles) nearly 35° east to about 75° west.

There are five climatic regions in Brazil:

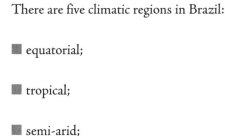 equatorial;

tropical;

semi-arid;

coastal;

sub-tropical.

Plateau cities such as São Paulo, Brasília, and Bello Horizonte have milder climates, averaging 17°C. The average annual temperature in the Amazonian rainforests is around 27°C and temperatures over 32°C are rare. Rio de Janeiro, Recife and Salvador on the coast have warm climates, balanced by the constancy of the Trade Winds.

In the south of Brazil (around Porto Alegre), the climate is sub-tropical and frost is not unknown. Here the seasons are more noticeable. In addition there are mountain ranges where snow and frost are often found. The hottest part of Brazil is the North East where, between May and November (the dry season), temperatures of 40°C have been recorded. Along the coast from Recife to Rio de Janeiro mean annual temperatures range from 23°C to 27°C.

The seasons in Brazil are the reverse of those in the northern hemisphere. Spring is from September 22nd to December 21st, summer from December 22nd to March 21st, autumn from March 22nd to June 21st and winter runs from June 22nd to September 21st.

The Amazon is the world's largest river in terms of volume of water and second longest (3,115 miles long), after the Nile. Of this 2,246 miles are in Brazil.

Chapter 2

The five regions of Brazil

Brazil is a country of amazing variety: from the Amazonian jungle to the Atlantic coast; from the plateaux, mountains and river basins to the major cities, Brazil really does have something for everyone.

The country is broken down into 26 states (*estados*) and one district containing the capital – Brasília. The states are based on historic borders. The country is also divided into five regions: North, North East, Central West, South East and South. In alphabetical order, the states are as follows:

Acre, Alagoas, Amapá, Amazonas, Bahia, Ceará, Espírito Santo, Goiás, Maranhão, Mato Grosso, Mato Grosso do Sul, Minas Gerais, Pará, Paraíba, Paraná, Pernambuco, Piauí, Rio de Janeiro, Rio Grande do Norte, Rio Grande do Sul, Rondônia, Roraima, Santa Catarina, São Paulo, Sergipe, Tocantins. In addition there is the Distrito Federal.

Below is a snapshot of information on each state within each region

NORTH REGION

The North region encompasses the states of Acre, Amapá, Amazonas, Pará, Rondônia, Roraima and Tocantins.

Acre

Acre is in the north west of Brazil and is largely Amazonian jungle. It is about the size of Tunisia or the state of Georgia in the USA. The capital city is Rio Branco meaning 'white river'. The city name derives from Baron Rio Branco who negotiated with Bolivia for the territory to attach to Brazil rather than Bolivia. It is inhabited mainly by indigenous people who speak one of the few remaining indigenous languages, Panoan. The Nukini Indians live on the banks of the Moa River.

The annual temperature for this state varies between 21°C to 32°C with an annual average temperature of 24°. However, it is always very humid.

The Serra do Divisor is a huge national park, covering over 846,000 hectares. It is a tropical paradise for the eco tourist. In particular, the Jurua Valley is a sanctuary surrounded by narrow waterways, river beaches of clear water, fine sand and preserved tropical forest.

In terms of relative wealth, it relies mainly upon the production and exportation of rubber. The state has some tourist infrastructure and accommodation is available in the city of Cruzeiro do Sul.

Amapá

Amapá lies in the extreme north, bordering French Guyana, at the mouth of the Amazon River and is largely rainforest. Its capital city is Macapa and the state of Amapá is roughly the size of Greece, but bigger than the state of New York. It is becoming one of the most popular destinations for the eco tourist.

The Equator crosses right through the state. Amapá is a perfect resting place for migratory birds as well as home to flamingos, toucans, guaras (a native South American bird) and sea and river turtles. It is also home to the alligator, the great anteater *tamandua-bandeira*, the giant armadillo *tatu-canastra* and many others. The state has very low levels of deforestation, at most 2%. Most of the state is forested with savannahs and plain areas. The coastal region is intact and includes swamps: the mix of salt and fresh water creates a perfect ecological paradise for many species of animals.

Over a quarter of the area of the state is protected and has native Indian reservations where over 5,000 of the Galibi, Karipuni, Palikur and Waiapi tribes live.

The economy of the state relies upon the production of iron, bauxite (used in the manufacture of aluminium) and other ores.

Amazonas

Amazonas, located in the north and bordering Peru, Colombia and Venezuela is the largest state in area in Brazil. The whole state has an area of 1,570,947 square kilometres and has a population of 3.3 million people. It is nearly the size of Iran or the state of Alaska.

Although it is mainly rainforest, the Amazon River basin cuts through the heart of the state and includes flood plains. Some trees found in the forest are over 20 metres in height but, in the main, the forest comprises shorter and denser flora and fauna making it difficult to penetrate.

The highest mountain in Brazil, Pico da Neblina (at 2,994m above sea level), is located in the National Park of Pico da Neblina. There are tours of the Amazon that go to other parks, such as the Ecological Park of January, which includes a canoe ride along a water-lily-covered river. Located in the area is the National Park of Jua which is the largest forest reserve of the continent. The city of Barceló is a popular place to stay whilst conducting a tour of the Amazon. There are also organised tours of the Reserve of Mamiraua and Humaita which provide sport fishing, forest hikes and overnight stays in forest lodges. Some of the lodges in the forest are either at the edge of a river or floating on a lake. The state holds music and dance festivals celebrating the cultural roots of the Amazon.

The capital city Manaus is an important centre for ecological tourism. One of the main attractions of the city of Manaus is the National Institute of Amazon Research (INPA) which houses a botanic garden rich in the flora of the Amazon, and a zoo with native species of animals of the Amazon, some of which are endangered.

The *Enterpe Oleracea* palm tree commonly known as the *acai* (pronounced ah-sigh-ee) grows in abundance in the Amazon. The trunk of the tree produces an ivory coloured, fibrous substance that is used in salads in Brazil. The tree also produces a fruit, the acai berry, which is very popular in Brazil as a superfood.

Pará

This is in the mid north of Brazil and borders Guyana and Suriname. It is larger than South Africa and over four times the size of the state of Arizona. The capital is Belém. The area falls largely within the Amazon rainforest and has a population of 7.1 million.

It was colonised by the Portuguese who built Castle Fortress at Guajara Bay, Belém. The Dutch and English invaded the state in search of various herbs and spices, notably pepper. They also wanted *guarana*, made from the seeds of a Brazilian shrub, which is used as a stimulant and annatto seed, which is used in cooking.

The state has countless islands, as well as lakes, beaches and mountains to offer, but is presently one of the biggest producers of iron, bauxite, manganese, limestone and tin as well as gold and has one of the largest gold mines, the Serra Pelada. It also exports these products to Europe and Japan. Pará is one of the richest states in Brazil and is also very strong in the agricultural industry with cattle rearing. Nearly one sixth of Brazil's exports originate from this state.

It is still home to over 40 indigenous groups, some of the largest of being the Andira Maraú, Munduruku and the Kayapo. Over eight million hectares within the state have been earmarked for indigenous groups and are preserved as such by FUNAI, the National Foundation of the Indian.

The state is also home to the largest festival celebrating the patron saint of Brazil, Our Lady of Nazareth, and many Brazilians pay homage by travelling to the state for the second Sunday of October.

Rondônia

This state lies in the north west and borders Bolivia. The capital city is Porto Velho and the state population is 1.6 million.

This area is mostly Amazon rainforest but, since the 1970s, about 60% has been deforested; that is to say 120,000 square kilometres. Its main activity is still, however, the exportation of wood.

Karipuna is a native language that is spoken by the Akuntsu race, living in this region. In 1995, there were 12 surviving members of the Akuntsu race; 11 years later, the members of the Akuntsu tribe were down to six.

Roraima

This is in the extreme north and borders Venezuela and Guyana. It is the size of Bulgaria and Cuba put together or comparable to the state of Minnesota. The equator bisects the state.

Its capital is Boa Vista and it's the least populated state with only 405,000 inhabitants. The annual mean temperature is 26°C and most of the area is within the Amazon rainforest. The state is still rich in gold, diamonds, cassiterite (a tin oxide and the chief tin ore of today), bauxite and copper.

The state has the largest indigenous population in Brazil, of which the Yanomami is the largest in number. Approximately 30,000 indigenous people live in the reserves specifically earmarked for them. The indigenous tribe, the Macuxi, are in conflict with the Yanomami over mineral deposits in the state.

The Monte Roraima National Park is situated 2,727 metres above sea level and includes one of Brazil's highest mountains, the Tepui Monte Roraima.

Tocantins

This is a land-locked state in the mid-north and is comparable in size to the state of Colorado. The capital is Palmas and the population of the state is 1.3 million. The economy is based on cattle-raising and pineapple plantations.

There are 20 archaeologically important sites and the area is becoming a major tourist site with camping facilities offering various leisure activities, including rafting. There is a plan to construct a north–south railway through Brazil – which would make Tocantins Brazil's fastest-growing state.

It is home to a large number of indigenous Indians and is now the centre for teaching and learning Indian language mother tongues; this has been recognised by UNESCO as a model for other countries to follow with an indigenous population.

NORTH EAST REGION

The North East region comprises the states of Alagoas, Bahia, Ceará, Maranhão, Paraíba, Pernambuco, Piauí, Rio Grande do Norte and Sergipe.

The North East coastal region is very popular with tourists. The hottest states in the North East region clockwise are Maranhão, Piauí, Ceará, Rio Grande do Norte, Paraíba, Pernambuco, Alagoas, Sergipe and Bahia.

Alagoas

This is a relatively small state in the North East region, between Pernambuco and Sergipe and is the same size as Haiti or the state of Massachusetts. The capital city is Maceió and the state has a population of just over three million people.

The racial makeup here is 97% white and 3% mixed. Historically, the state relied mainly on the production of sugar cane and tobacco for its economy, but in the recent past it diversified and now has more of a manufacturing base, including oil and gas, agro-business producing pineapples, rice, beans, tobacco, cassava, coconut and corn. It also has vast reserves of rock salt.

Bahia

Bahia, pronounced 'Baa'eea', is the most southerly of the states on the north eastern coast. The capital city is Salvador with a population of nearly 14 million. It is bigger than France and comparable in size to the state of Texas.

This is the fourth most populous state in Brazil and 62% of its population is of mixed race, but only 0.5% is indigenous.

This is the main producer of cacao which is used to make cocoa and chocolate, although tourism is a very large part of its economy.

Ceará

This state is located between Piauí and Rio Grande do Norte on the north eastern coast and its capital is Fortaleza. In terms of size it is bigger than Nepal, and comparable in size to the state of Iowa. It has a population of 8.2 million.

It has a very varied environment and lies between the Brazilian highlands and the sandy coastal plain. It has mangroves, jungle, scrubland and tropical forest. The long dry season results in much of the scrubland being barren and brown.

The large beaches are a major tourist attraction. The uplands are dry and hot in the day, but cool at night. There is a rainy season from January to June.

Maranhão

This state neighbours Piauí on the north eastern coast and is the size of Vietnam or twice the size of the state of Georgia in the USA. It has a population of 6.2 million and its capital, São Luis, is a World Heritage Site with three thousand buildings, erected between the 17th and 19th centuries during Brazil's colonial period.

The northern part of the state is forested and the southern part is in the Brazilian highlands. The state relies on the production of many species of palm, which is a major source of revenue for the state, as well as agri-business including timber. The state does not suffer with droughts as it has a rainy season.

Paraíba

This state neighbours Pernambuco and Rio Grande do Norte on the north eastern coast. The capital is João Pessoa and the state population is 3.6 million. The Portuguese, French and Dutch settled in the state from the beginning of the 16th century and each have left their mark, not just in the way of rich architecture, but also in the appearance of its population.

The state produces mainly leather products, beef, sugar cane and the finest tourmaline crystals. Tourism is also a major industry.

Pernambuco

This state has a narrow coastal area and neighbours Alagoas and Paraíba. The coastal strip was once covered by a forest, but this has been replaced with sugar cane plantations. The capital is Recife and the state population is about 8.5 million.

In the centre of the state there are still semi-deciduous Pernambuco forests. Pernambuco is a reddish, tropical, hardwood much sought after for its appearance and qualities which are favoured for, amongst other things, violin bows and cabinet making.

Pernambuco was the site of internal unrest and insurrections in the 19th century and a revolution in 1817 when there was a purported declaration of independence by rebels, following the lead of the USA and France. This was the first attempt to establish a Brazil independent of Portuguese government.

The main industries here are the growing of sugar cane and its conversion into alcohol for both human consumption (in the form of a white rum called Cachaca, pronounced 'cashassa') and motor fuel, although there is probably little difference in the taste between the two! Tourism is also a major source of revenue.

Piauí

This state neighbours Maranhao and Ceará in the north east with a short coastline and is the size of the United Kingdom. The capital is Teresina and the state population is three million.

There are important archaeological sites in this state dating from pre-historic Amerindian civilisation. It is devoid of any industry and is a natural paradise, with numerous islands, lagoons, brooks, fine sand beaches, sand dunes and vast numbers of coconut trees. The state relies on cattle rearing and growing varied species of the palm tree for its economy.

Rio Grande do Norte

This state neighbouring Ceará and Paraíba is dominated by the coastline and is famous for its beaches and sand dunes. It is also said to have the cleanest air in South America. The capital city is Natal and the state population is three million.

Until the 1980s, sugar and cattle raising provided livelihoods, but since then tourism has become of major importance. It still produces 70% of Brazil's melons and great quantities of mangoes and cashews (the nuts which grow on delicious edible fruits that can also be made into juice). The state is also home to the world's largest cashew tree, which was planted in 1888. The tree spreads out to cover 7,300 square metres producing 80,000 cashews a year!

The ocean waters are laden with salt which is harvested. In the 1970s petroleum was discovered in Natal and it is now the biggest land-based producer in Brazil.

Sergipe

This state neighbours Alagoas and Bahia and is the smallest of all 26 states. The capital is Aracaju and the state population is two million.

Inland, the state is savannah and the coastline comprises mangroves, swamps and sandy beaches. It relies mainly on the production of sugar cane (producing 1.4 million tons of sugar annually), and has some income from tourism.

In the 1930s outlaws were there; amongst them Virgolino Ferreira da Silva – 'The King of Bandits' who terrorized the state for a decade, he was later beheaded by the police and his head was displayed on a pole in a village square.

CENTRAL WEST REGION

The Central West region includes the states of Distrito Federal, Goiás, Mato Grosso and Mato Grosso do Sul.

Distrito Federal

This is the state department, which houses the country's modern capital of Brasília which was built very quickly between 1960 and 1964. It is a land-locked area, bordering Goiás and Minas Gerais. It has a population of 2.4 million and an economy which relies on service industries and the provision of administrative resources. The population is a mixture of 44% white, 48% mixed race and 6% black.

Goiás

Goiás lies in the centre of Brazil in the Brazilian highlands and has a population of 5.75 million. It is larger than Finland and twice the size of the state of Florida.

The state was very prosperous during the colonial era as it was a magnet for gold prospecting and many of the buildings in the state are reminders of its rich heritage.

Nowadays the land is used for cattle and fowl rearing and it boasts around 18 million head of cattle and 80 million fowl. There is also mineral production and food processing.

Mato Grosso

This is in the south western part of Brazil and borders Bolivia to the south west. It is nearly as big as Venezuela and larger than the states of New Mexico, Arizona and Nevada put together.

The name means 'thick jungle' and is the site of some of the worst deforestation in the world. It is a farming state consisting of cattle rearing. The Bororo Indians live in this region amongst a total population of 2.9 million. The remoteness of the area led Captain Percy Fawcett (1867–1925) to search for lost cities: it is here that he disappeared – maybe because it is said to be the location of access to the interior of the earth in hollow earth theories.

Pantanal is an area in this state. It is home to a known 3,500 species of plant, 650 species of bird, 400 species of fish, 100 species of mammal and 80 species of reptile. It measures 68,000 square miles and is one of the world's most productive habitats. Annual floods, fed by tropical rains create a giant nursery for aquatic life. As the waters recede in the dry season, the Pantanal attracts a great influx of birds and other creatures. Considered to be one of the hemisphere's greatest phenomena, the bird species are particularly diverse. The region is an important migratory stop-over point, used by birds from three major migratory flyways, bringing ospreys from the Antarctic areas, wood storks from the Argentine Pampas in the south and flycatchers from the Andes in the west.

The Pantanal is a paradise for naturalists, photographers and tourists. The density of wildlife is considered to be the largest in the tropics; even greater than Amazonia. This includes the highest population of crocodiles in the world, with numbers put at ten million. In the 1970s one million skins a year were illegally poached. The Pantanal continues to be the best place to see jaguars, giant river otters, giant anteaters, armadillos, the endangered maned wolf and marsh deer.

There have been 15 species of parrot identified in the region, including the blue and yellow macaw, the blue-fronted Amazon, the green-winged macaw and the red-shouldered macaw. The Pantanal remains one of the best environments to see the endangered hyacinth macaw; the largest member of the parrot family. Many reports have also put the scarlet macaw in the state of Mato Grosso.

Other species commonly encountered include the anaconda, howler monkey, capucine monkey, ocelot, cougar, tapir, great egret, snowy egret, rosette spoonbill and the jaburu stork (the symbol of the Pantanal).

Hunting is proscribed throughout Brazil. With its variety of ecological landscapes, from terrestrial forests, seasonally inundated grasslands to perennial lakes, the Pantanal is a complex of ecosystems.

Threats to the Pantanal from human activities include uncontrolled recreational fishing, illegal hunting and smuggling of endangered species. Despite this, the government of Brazil is encouraging tourism here.

Mato Grosso do Sul

Mato Grosso do Sul is in the south west and borders Paraguay and Bolivia; it is larger than Germany and the state of New Mexico. Its name means 'southern thick jungle'.

It has a population of 2.3 million and the capital is Campo Grande. The economic wealth of this state is primarily through farming.

There is a growing tourist trend which is mainly in the city of Bonito where there are many huge grottos and caves. The state is also home to the South Pantanal: see above for more information.

SOUTH EAST REGION

The South East region includes the states of Espírito Santo, Minas Gerais, Rio de Janeiro and São Paulo.

Espírito Santo

This neighbours Minas Gerais to the west and Bahia to the north, its capital being Vitória. It is larger than Denmark and twice the size of the state of New Jersey. It has a population of 3.5 million, some of whom are the indigenous people called

Capixabas. There is a big German, Italian, Spanish and Gypsy influence in this state.

The state does not as yet have a great influx of tourism despite its natural beauty and its architecturally-rich history in the cities of Vitória and Vila Velha, founded in 1534.

Minas Gerais

This is in the western part of the south east, completely landlocked and is the second most populous state, being bigger than Kenya in Africa or, France and is twice the size of the state of Colorado. Its capital is Belo Horizonte and the state population is 19.5 million. It is famed for many colonists seeking gold and gems, including diamonds.

It has a more native culture than its neighbouring states such as São Paulo and Rio de Janeiro, which are altogether more cosmopolitan, although there has been a great influx of Italians and central Europeans. It is regarded as being the most religious state, with a mix of Roman Catholic and Evangelical churches.

The great Brazilian footballer Pelé comes from this state. Over half of the population are of Portuguese or Italian descent and a third are of mixed race. It is a great producer of milk, coffee and electronic goods, as well as minerals. Fiat and Mercedes Benz have factories there. The north east of this state is relatively poor, but attracts foreign traders for the semi-precious stones such as topaz, aquamarine, amethyst and tourmaline. There are many immigrants from this state who have settled in Boston, USA.

Rio de Janeiro

This is not just the famous city of the carnival (before Brasília was built, virtually overnight in 1960, it was the old capital), but also a state in the south east of the country with a famous coastline and landmarks. It neighbours São Paulo and is the size of Switzerland and nearly twice the size of New Jersey.

Its tropical climate is home to 15.6 million people. The population is about half white European (Italian and German) and *mulattos* – people of mixed origin – account for over a third. Amerindians account for 0.3% and 10% are black. The state boasts both mountains and plains and the coast is carved by the bays of

Guanabara, Ilha Grande and Sepetiba. There are forests, lagoons and dense vegetation. Surprisingly, there is also room for agriculture, comprising production of sugar cane and coffee. The capital city is an important port, exporting crude oil and steel. It is also a cultural centre with theatres, cinemas, an opera house, luxurious hotels and cosmopolitan restaurants.

Tourism is flourishing owing to the grand setting of the city and its famous landmarks: the Sugar Loaf Mountain, the statue of Christ as well as Copacabana and Ipanema beaches. Also in the state is the historic city of Petrópolis in the mountains and along the coast there are the tourist cities of Angra dos Reis, Cabo Frio and the isthmus of Búzios (made famous in the 1960s by a short visit from Brigitte Bardot). Other cities along the stretch of coast known as the region of the lakes (really enormous sea-fed lagoons), such as Saquarema are encouraging tourism. People of the city of Rio are known as *Cariocas* and those in the rest of the state are called *Fluminenses*.

São Paulo

This state neighbours Rio de Janeiro to the north and Paraná state to the south. It is larger than the United Kingdom. The capital is the city of São Paulo and the population of the state is 41.1 million. It is the most populous country sub-division in the western hemisphere.

This is the richest state in Brazil; manufacturing cars and aeroplanes as well as commodities such as textiles, oranges, sugar cane and coffee. São Paulo also provides services to the financial and commercial industry. The GDP for the state is US$550 billion a year, making it one of the biggest economies in Latin America.

The population is the most diverse in Brazil, including: fifteen million of Italian descent, seven million of Spanish descent, five million of Lebanese and Syrian descent and four million Japanese (the largest Japanese population outside of Japan).

SOUTH REGION

The South region comprises the states Paraná, Rio Grande do Sul and Santa Catarina.

Paraná

This is the most northerly state of the South region, in part neighbouring the state of Santa Catarina and bordering Paraguay and Argentina. The capital is Curitiba and the state has a population of 10.4 million.

It was settled by gold prospectors and three quarters of the population are white European originally from Germany, Italy, Poland and the Ukraine. Early in the 20th century there was a wave of immigration from Japan, the Lebanon and Syria.

Its thriving agri-business produces wheat, corn, soy beans, potatoes and coffee. It has 8.5 million cattle producing 1.3 billion litres of milk a year. Apart from agri-business, it is home to an industrial park housing 24,000 companies. Curitiba is a major business tourism destination for those in search of investment opportunities.

Paraná has 220,000 hectares of the Iguaçu National Park (50,000 hectares is in Argentina), a UNESCO world heritage site. The word *iguaçu* means large water in the Tupi-Guarani language. The Iguaçu National Park is a major tourist destination for Brazilians and foreigners alike. The biggest attraction being the waterfalls at Garganta do Diabo (meaning devil's throat), which are on the Argentinean side. There are helicopter tours available to see the full glory of these falls.

Other attractions in Paraná include an eco-museum; Zoologico Bosque Guarani (the Guarani Woods Zoo) spread across 40,000 square metres, which is home to roughly 50 mammal species, 350 bird species and 250 butterfly species; The Three Borders Landmark (Brazil, Argentina and Paraguay); the Itaipu hydro-electric plant, the largest in the world of its kind and Parque das Aves (the Bird Park) with 900 birds of 180 species from all over the world. The Bird Park also has a dedicated butterfly sanctuary with 25 species and a separate reptile sector.

For the golf enthusiast there is an 18-hole professional golf course stretching over 600 square metres at 'The Bourbon Iguaçu Golf Club and Resort' which has a complete leisure and lodging infrastructure and draws sports enthusiasts from all over Brazil.

Rio Grande do Sul

This state is the most southerly of the states of Brazil and is the size of New Zealand. The capital, Porto Alegre, has many business centres, hotels, shopping malls, music theatres, and a good international airport. The population of Rio Grande do Sol is 11 million.

The state attracts many kinds of tourism:

■ business;

■ rural, including the traditional Gaucho farms;

■ ecological;

■ religious, attracting half a million people a year;

■ historical-cultural.

There are specific resorts to deal with particular tourist trades, such as The Hydro Mineral Resort providing trails for hiking and horseback riding, the production of arts and crafts made of wicker, rattan and wood as well as resorts for fishing on the Uruguay River. The Jacui River is one of the largest in the state, with a course of nearly 300 miles.

The Pampas area comprises large farms, and in the Gaucho Pampas one can find rodeos and fandangos. The famous footballer Ronaldinho Gaucho comes from this state.

Santa Catarina

This state is on the Atlantic coast neighbouring Rio Grande do Sul and Paraná. It borders Argentina and is the size of Portugal or Indiana State. The capital is Florianópolis and the state population is six million.

Santa Catarina is regarded as the most European-influenced state in Brazil: the people are descendants of Portuguese, German and Italian immigrants. It is said to enjoy the highest standard of living in Brazil. 92% of the population is white, and 35% are of German descent; 30% are Italian; 22% are Portuguese and 5% are Polish, Russian and Norwegian; 8% are classed'other'. Tourism is its biggest source of revenue.

Chapter 3

Visas

Like it or not, visas will have to be applied for by most people who visit Brazil. Here's the vital information you'll need to ease the process.

There are seven main types of visas, which permit entry into Brazil:

- tourist;

- business;

- technical;

- student;

- cultural;

- investor;

- retirement;

- permanent.

We will deal with each in turn.

TOURIST VISAS

Citizens of the countries listed below are exempt from the requirement to apply for a tourist visa to visit Brazil. However, such visas (or exemptions) permit entry for 90 days and for limited purposes, which are described below. If the purpose of your visit includes anything outside the usual meaning of 'tourism', you will need to apply for a different type.

Procedure for exempt countries

Exempt countries include:

- Andorra, Argentina, Austria, Bahamas, Barbados, Belgium, Bermuda, Bolivia, Chile, Columbia, Costa Rica, Denmark, Ecuador, Finland, France, Germany, Great Britain, Greece, Iceland, Italy, Liechtenstein, Luxembourg, Malaysia, Monaco, Morocco, Namibia, Netherlands, Norway, Paraguay, Peru, Philippines, Portugal, San Marino, Slovenia, South Africa, Spain, Surinam, Sweden, Switzerland, Trinidad and Tobago, Uruguay, Vatican State, Venezuela.

Extensions may be granted, subject to a small fee, by the Delegacia de Estrangeiros (Foreigners' Department) in the local office of the Policia Federal (Federal Police), for a further period of 90 days in any 12-month period from first entry into Brazil. It is permissible to make multiple entries on these visas. If you apply for this extension, make sure that you take with you:

- your passport;

- your return flight ticket;

- your disembarkation card;

- a valid international credit card (or other proof of means);

- the name of someone whom you have met in Brazil who would be prepared to speak for you, should the need arise.

Remember that Brazilian bureaucracy is slow, but it is carried out according to the book. If you forget one of the documents, mentioned above, you will probably be turned away. You would then need to return with all the correct paperwork or become 'irregular'. An irregular over-stayer in Brazil is *not* an illegal immigrant. It just means that the Policia Federal *may* serve a notice on you to leave the country within eight days from the date of the notice. If you disobey such a notice, *then* you become illegal and may be subject to deportation. Moreover, in any event, for every day that you over-stay, you are subject to a fine on leaving of R$8 (c£2.40) per day, subject to a maximum of 100 days – a grand total of R$800 (c£240) per person. There is a little-known judicial discretion, exercisable by the judges, to extend a temporary visa by up to 60 days from its prospective expiry date. However, this discretion is exercised very sparingly and is intended to meet wholly exceptional circumstances.

Procedure for non-exempt countries

Non-exempt countries include:

■ Australia, Canada, Japan, Mexico, Nigeria, Poland, Russia, South Korea, USA.

Application forms are available on the websites of the Brazilian Consulates in the countries concerned. To find the websites just search 'Brazilian Consulate' and then the capital city of your country. The fees vary somewhat, but are in the region of US$30–110. You will need to submit a passport with at least six months to run, an application form, a passport photograph, and a copy of a return ticket showing dates. Moreover, if you are not staying in a hotel, you will need to send a notarised invitation letter (available from a public notary), from your host stating his or her citizenship or visa status, occupation and address, how and when they first met you and details of your intended activities in Brazil. Lecturers need to send a signed letter of invitation from a Brazilian institution. If you are married to a Brazilian citizen, you must produce your marriage certificate. Applications by minors must be signed by both parents whose signatures must be notarised. Sometimes, too, there is a service fee per passport processed.

BUSINESS VISAS

The applicant will need a passport valid for at least six months from their arrival in Brazil and with at least two blank pages left; an application form can be down-loaded from the website of the Brazilian Consulate General in their home country. This needs to be completed and signed, accompanied by a recent passport photograph and a business letter from the applicant's company, addressed to the Consulate of Brazil, stating:

- the employer's details;

- the job and title of the applicant;

- the precise purpose and description of the applicant's assignment in Brazil;

- the financial responsibility of the applicant;

- dates of stay;

- name and address of the organisation to be visited;

- name and title of contact person in Brazil.

The letter must be signed by a company official.

There must also be an invitation letter from the Brazilian company, which must be on the company letterhead, addressed to the Consulate of Brazil in the applicant's home country stating the purpose of the trip to Brazil. The letter must be signed and include the signatory's job title, job description and company address.

Fees for a business visa depend on the country of origin. In the USA there is a visa fee of US$170 per passport and a service fee per passport – in the USA the service fee is US$60 per passport.

TECHNICAL VISAS

Technical visas are issued for 30 or 90 days, or even 12 months, where it is shown that there is an executed contract for services between the home country employer company and the host company in Brazil. A technical work visa is issued on the basis that the employment is not remunerated directly by the Brazilian host company and forms the basis of technical input to the Brazilian host company for a short and specified length of time by the individual concerned.

The procedure for these is the same as for the business visa, except that the applicant needs to download two application forms and provide two photographs and the Ministry of Labour in Brazil must approve the applicant's visit. Only after approval has been granted can the process of obtaining a technical visa start.

Fees for technical visas vary, again, according to country of origin, but in the USA it is US$210 per passport plus a service fee of US$60.

STUDENT VISAS

Passport requirements are the same as for tourist and business visas. Two application forms must be downloaded and completed and two passport photographs provided. All applicants over 16 years of age must provide a signed good conduct police report from their country of origin. The letter must originate from the main police department from the city in which the applicant has resided for the past year. The report must be dated within 90 days of the application.

The fee for a student visa is payable according to country of origin. In the USA it is US$150 per passport plus a service fee of US$60.

Each student needs a consent/authorisation letter from both parents or legal guardians; the signatures must be notarised by a public notary.

There must be an enrolment letter from a Brazilian Government Agency or an authorised academic institution, or a letter of invitation from an international co-operation organisation confirming:

■ the applicant's acceptance or registration;

■ enrolment situation;

■ description of courses and activities, scholarship or means of support;

■ names, addresses and qualifications of any persons who will be financially responsible for the applicant while in Brazil.

Anyone without a scholarship or financial aid must show proof of means of support. The Consulate accepts bank statements, family financial support letters or documents showing other sources of income.

There must be proof of international health insurance.

There must be a signed letter from a university, school or other academic institution in the country of origin, on an official letterhead, explaining the precise purpose of the study or course and whether it is part of the student's curriculum programme, including a statement of financial responsibility for the applicant while in Brazil.

The applicant must include a copy of a round trip ticket reservation or e-ticket reservation.

CULTURAL VISAS

The passport requirements are the same as above. There must be two application forms (downloadable from the website of the Brazilian Consulate General in the applicant's home country) and two passport photographs, together with a letter from the applicant's sponsor, including a statement of financial responsibility whilst in Brazil and the letter must be on the sponsor's letterhead. Originals must be supplied and a fax copy is not acceptable. If the applicant is to remain for more than 90 days, there must be a police record check issued by the applicant's local police department. The fee for the visa varies from country to country, but for the USA it is US$170 per passport plus a service fee of US$60.

INVESTOR VISAS

Brazil's National Immigration Council (NIC) lowered the amount of investment needed for obtaining a permanent residency in Brazil to US$50,000 on 6th October 2004. This investment can be made by investing in real estate and by satisfying certain conditions. The investor needs a copy of their passport, proof of address in their home country and a power of attorney to enable the process to be begun in Brazil. The usual method is to form a Brazilian company, following which a bank account is opened. US$50,000 is transferred from the investor's account abroad to a new corporate account in Brazil. In order to begin this process it is necessary to apply for a Brazilian tax number (called a CPF number). Banco Central do Brasil (the regulatory state bank) issues a certificate proving that the money has been brought from abroad, after which the visa application is filed in Brazil and, once approved by the Ministry of Labour, the visa will be issued to the Brazilian Consulate in the country of origin for collection by the applicant in person. Entry to Brazil with the visa must be effected within 90 days of issue. The visa is subject to review after five years.

It is certainly advisable to have professional advice in relation to these processes. The Consulates-General of countries represented in Brazil often have lists of professionals who can help with the technicalities involved.

RETIREMENT VISAS

Applicants for a permanent retirement visa must be over 50 years of age and must be able to prove a monthly pension of the equivalent to US$2,000 for up to two people. For each extra dependent, an extra US$1,000 income per month must be shown. Applicants must provide:

■ an authenticated copy of their passport(s) (i.e. notarised before a public notary);

■ a certified copy of each person's birth certificate;

■ any marriage certificate;

■ evidence from a local police department that the applicant has no criminal record;

■ a notarised letter from the institution responsible for paying the retirement pension;

■ a notarised declaration from the applicant's local bank agency that they will transfer the pension to a bank account in Brazil.

There is a charge by the Brazilian Consulate in the applicant's home country of the equivalent of US$20 for each document. Once the visa is approved, the applicant must attend the Brazilian Consulate General in the applicant's home country to have the visa issued. They will need: their passport; two passport photographs; two visa application forms and a visa fee, which in the USA is US$200. If the applicant does not attend in person there is a US$10 absence fee. The first entry to Brazil must be made within 90 days of issue and the applicants must register with the Federal police within 30 days of first entering Brazil. If the applicant leaves Brazil for a period of two years or more, the visa expires.

PERMANENT VISAS

Apart from the investor and retirement visas mentioned above, there are several other means of obtaining permanent residency in Brazil, as listed below.

1. The applicant must be a researcher or high level professional specialist, showing a document from a Brazilian research institution manifesting its interest in the services of the researcher, a CV and appropriate academic references and diplomas.

2. The applicant must be an administrator, manager or director of a start-up company, which means a non-Brazilian company which has been in business outside Brazil for at least five years preceding the application. The foreign company must give a power of attorney to its new legal representatives in Brazil, to set up the company in Brazil.

3. The applicant must be the administrator, manager or director of a professional or business corporation. This category covers inter-company transfers.

4. The applicant must be married to a Brazilian citizen and apply to the Ministry of Justice, via the Regional Federal Police Office, or to a Brazilian Consulate abroad and provide evidence of the matrimonial union. Immigration officials will carry out a surprise visit to the couple's home, to ensure that the marriage is not a marriage of convenience, the principal purpose of which is fraudulently to obtain a residence visa.

5. The applicant must be a foreigner with Brazilian offspring. Application is made to the Ministry of Justice via the Regional Federal Police Office or to a Brazilian Consulate abroad. The offspring should be economically dependent on the applicant and be under their guardianship.

6. The applicant must be able to show that they are joining a family member who is a Brazilian citizen or holder of a Brazilian permanent visa. The applicant's spouse and unmarried children under 21 years or 24 if in higher education, an incapacitated child, an unmarried orphaned sibling under 21, a grandchild or great grandchild, an under-24 unmarried orphaned sibling in higher education, an incapacitated sibling, grandchild or great grandchild, or the applicant's parents may also be covered.

Chapter 4

Why buy real estate in Brazil?

The first question is why buy real estate in Brazil at all and, ancillary to that, for what personal objective? We deal with this here. The second question is where to buy? (See Chapter 5) The third is how to buy? (See Chapter 6)

WHY BUY?

There are many general reasons for buying real estate in Brazil; whether to live there more or less full time, as a holiday destination or as an investment or rental opportunity. The first general reason is that, in comparison with western economies, it is extremely cheap. It is cheap because, despite the presence of the internationally active HSBC, mortgage-lending has not caught on. This, in turn, results from the fact that interest rates in Brazil on borrowed money are high – somewhere around a minimum of 1% *per month* is payable by the banks for money invested with them – in comparison with between 3–8% *per annum* in North America and Western Europe. Plainly, when they lend money out, they charge more than this and so people cannot afford long-term borrowing.

Accordingly, prices are geared to the local economy and the ability to pay and it is not unusual to be able to purchase a house and land for a twentieth of the cost of a comparable property in North America or Western Europe. This means that, for an investment of US$100,000, you can get a house which, in any reasonable location in North America or Western Europe, would set you back US$2,000,000 – and the North American and European equivalents probably would not be as well built (even allowing for the Brazilian weakness for plugs and bare electrical wires in bathrooms, showers and even in the garden).

Typical Brazilian houses are built to last. They are largely built with concrete and, unlike many buildings in Western Europe and the USA, do not include timber or plasterboard. Near the thundering and windswept south Atlantic coast houses need to be strong: there is no room for shoddy workmanship, skimping on materials or the use of kiln-dried or unseasoned soft woods.

In the Brazilian economy, people design and build their own houses. That being said, there are increasing numbers of companies which specialise in building 'condominiums' for foreigners or 'Gringos' who are too afraid to immerse themselves in the society in which they have chosen to live.

How does a local Brazilian bank manager, on say, R$1,000 a month (c£240), manage to build his own house? Through thrift and by buying a plot of land and then building the house gradually, as time and circumstance allow.

It is well to bear in mind that currencies fluctuate and for that reason and for the fact that the Brazilian Real aligns itself as much as possible to the USD, references are made to the USD rather than the euro, British pound or any other currency, where possible. It is also important to bear in mind that a purchaser will find that all monies transferred into Brazil for house purchase (and cash withdrawals in Brazil) will be converted first to the USD and then to the Brazilian Real.

WHY INVEST IN BRAZIL?

There is another important factor in deciding to invest in Brazil. Many economists refer to Brazil, Russia, India and China as the likely world economic leaders in the current century. In Brazil's case this results from the fact that it still has enormous natural reserves and a wealth of renewable resources such as timber, sugar cane, coffee, fruit etc. Most important of all, there has been the discovery of oil on and off shore.

This is having profound influences, especially on the local coastal economies which are due royalties for the extraction of the oil. Once the 'usual deductions' have been made and have slipped neatly into back pockets, there will still be enough left to improve the towns along the Atlantic seaboard.

With improvements in the infrastructure will come tourism and the better shops and restaurants, which tourists, investors and immigrants will demand. At the moment there is a big difference between, say, a town such as Saquarema in Rio de Janeiro – with its wonderful landscape and setting, but poor roads and pavements and no top-notch shops, bars or restaurants – and the equally spectacular Búzios, a little to the north – 'discovered' by Brigitte Bardot in the 1960s and popularised overnight. Búzios has everything that a tourist could want: from a cinema, to a variety of restaurants, clothes' shops, good tobacconists, jewellery and even furniture shops.

With similar improvements in other areas such as Saquarema, land prices will, inevitably, swiftly increase, not least because more and more foreigners will bring their money and purchasing-power into the equation.

In brief, then, there are many sound economic reasons for buying land in Brazil.

Chapter 5

Where to buy real estate

With a wide variety of regions to choose from and a range of prices to suit every pocket, making this choice will not be easy.

There are three main coastal regions that appeal to newcomers and investors alike:

- the South East region – comprising the states of Rio de Janeiro and São Paulo;

- the North East region – comprising the states of Bahia, Alagoas, Pernambuco, Paraíba, Rio Grande do Norte and Ceará;

- the South region, comprising the states of Paraná, Santa Catarina and Rio Grande do Sul.

We will deal with each region in turn in this chapter. Note that prices listed are current at the time of writing when the R$1 was worth £0.301 or US$0.598. Some websites referred to in this chapter advertise properties for sale in GB£, US$ or the Brazilian R$.

THE SOUTH EAST

Rio de Janeiro

Rio is called the 'wonderful city' for very obvious reasons and is increasingly being used to host international events, thereby opening up the splendour of the city to the world. Apart from the beaches, which are an integral part of a Brazilian's life, there are many magnificent buildings and other attractions for those wishing to make Rio their home, some of which are listed in this book (see Chapter 9).

The world-famous beaches of Rio are markedly different from each other.

1. Ipanema Beach is probably the most famous in the world boasting beach soccer and volleyball. It has hosted the world championships for beach volleyball.

2. Copacabana Beach is also world famous and hosts the most famous New Year's Eve party in the country.

3. Leblon Beach is a calm beach with sports facilities including a cycle track.

4. Paianha Beach is a surfing beach surrounded by hilly Atlantic forests.

5. Grumari Beach has cliffs and an unspoilt beach with good surfing waves.

6. Arpoador Beach is famous for the rock that separates Copacabana and Ipanema Beaches.

7. Pepino Beach has the strongest surfing waves in Rio de Janeiro and is used for landing by hang-gliders.

8. Barra da Tijuca Beach has strong waves and is good for surfing.

9. Botafogo Beach is polluted, but has spectacular views towards Corcovado Hill and Sugar Loaf Mountain.

10. Flamengo Beach is also polluted even though it has calm waters and has views of the boats docked at Gloria Marina.

The main central areas of the city of Rio de Janeiro are divided into zones; 'Downtown' or Centro; 'South Zone' or 'Zona Sul' and the 'North Zone, Zona Norte.' Centro is the main commercial and business centre; the North Zone is industrialised and considered the poorer neighbour and the South Zone is inhabited by the well-heeled.

Centro
Centro is the historical centre of Rio and is now home to numerous museums; it is more particularly the business and financial hub of Rio. Real estate is

experiencing a comeback in the Santa Teresa neighbourhood in Centro. Santa Teresa has some of the most beautiful houses, architecturally, and you can buy a colonial style mansion there for around US$600,000 – but be aware that you will be cheek by jowl with *favelas* (squatter settlements) all around, which means that you need extra security and be prepared to stay in at night or use private transport with great caution.

The South Zone

The South Zone is the main residential area of Rio. The Atlantic coast consists of several beach districts, starting at Leme at one end and continuing down the coast via Copacabana, Arpoador, Ipanema, Leblon, and São Conrado.

Guanabara Bay is bordered by the districts of Gloria, Flamengo, Botafogo and Urca.

Other notable districts in the South Zone include Gavea, Jardim Botanico, Lagoa, Humaita, Laranjeiras, and Cosme Velho.

The real estate on the Atlantic coast comes at a premium for uninterrupted views of the ocean and more importantly, the cool breeze.

Copacabana and Leme

Copacabana and Leme have many of the large international hotels. Copacabana has a deep stretch of beach measuring approximately 4km in length. Nestled amongst the hotels are apartment blocks. Running parallel to Avenida Atlantica, is Avenida Senhora Nossas Copacabana, the main shopping street of Copacabana, which has many shopping malls, bars and restaurants. Some parts of Copacabana are sleazy, although others, such as the area around the Copacabana Palace Hotel, are not. Copacabana also has four slum areas.

Leme is so called as a nearby rock resembles the helm of a ship. The world-famous *Le Meridien* hotel is in this district, but is now known as the *Iberostar Hotel*.

- A two bedroom apartment in this area with one en suite bathroom, separate family bathroom, kitchen and one parking space in a condominium comes with a price tag of R$320,000.

- A three bedroom apartment in this area is available at R$550,000.

- A four bedroom apartment in this area with an extra bathroom measuring 220 square metres is available at R$750,000.

- An ocean view apartment comes at a cost: two bedroom apartments start at R$850,000 and four bedroom apartments, measuring approximately 370 square metres, including four parking spaces and ocean views, range from R$1,500,000 to around R$3,500,000.

- If a penthouse is what you are after, a small three bedroom apartment is available for R$350,000 and a five bedroom penthouse for R$1,500,000.

Ipanema

Ipanema district was probably made internationally famous by the song sung by Antonio Carlos Jobim and covered by Frank Sinatra's recording of the song *The Girl from Ipanema*. The word Ipanema is a Tupi word meaning 'bad water for fishing'. It was the estate that once belonged to the Baron of Ipanema. Although it is next door to Copacabana, it does not have a sleazy side and is a safe neighbourhood attracting the middle and upper classes. Property prices reflect this.

- A two bedroom apartment measuring 123 square metres in this area is available for R$485,000. A three bedroom apartment with two bathrooms comes with a price tag of R$650,000. A three bedroom apartment near to the beach can fetch R$700,000. A sunny four bedroom apartment with sea view fetches R$755,000.

- A one bedroom apartment with all rooms facing the ocean measuring only 87 square metres comes with a price tag of R$1,700,000 with shared leisure facilities in the block. A two bedroom ocean-front apartment measuring 216 square metres fetches R$2,300,000. A three/four bedroom ocean-front apartment fetches between R$2,500,000 and R$3,500,000.

- A two bedroom penthouse is available for as little as R$600,000; a three to four bedroom penthouse ranges from R$2,000,000 to R$2,600,000.

■ If you really must have a house, there is a four bedroom house with two maids' rooms, garage for two cars, measuring 420 square metres with a pool, for R$3,800,000.

Arpoador

Arpoador, meaning 'harpoon thrower', is an affluent area between Copacabana and Ipanema and is very peaceful. Property prices are similar to Ipanema.

Leblon

Leblon is also a very affluent area and more exclusive than Ipanema, although it attracts families and is considered less hip and trendy than its neighbour Ipanema. It is home to many exclusive and sophisticated cafés and restaurants, bookstores and shops. It was once the estate of a French plantation owner 'Le Blond'.

■ A two bedroom, one bathroom apartment measuring 80 square metres is being sold for R$380,000. Three bedroom apartments measuring 110 square metres upwards are available from R$520,000 to R$650,000.

■ A two bedroom apartment, measuring 119 square metres, with views of the Corcovado Mountain is fetching R$900,000. A three bedroom apartment with mountain and ocean views and with lots of marble in the interior is available at R$950,000. A similar four bedroom apartment is available for R$1,200,000.

■ A large three bedroom apartment measuring 326 square metres with three suites on two floors is available for R$1,900,050. A smaller four bedroom apartment measuring 211 square metres fetches R$2,200,000. A very large apartment measuring 395 square metres is available for R$3,000,000.

■ Three bedroom penthouses are available for R$850,000 rising to R$2,700,000. A four bedroom penthouse starts at R$1,700,000 rising to R$4,000,000.

São Conrado

São Conrado is a sophisticated neighbourhood for the wealthy of Rio. It has one of the largest shopping malls in Brazil with over 150 stores including designer shops. São Conrado also has a golf course and attracts wealthy residents despite being next to Rio's biggest *favela* which clings to the side of the mountain, Morro Dois Irmaos.

■ A very small one bedroom apartment measuring 59 square metres fetches R$160,000. A large two bedroom apartment fetches R$550,000, and a small four bedroom apartment can fetch the same price.

■ A large three bedroom apartment measuring 300 square metres with a lovely view fetches R$800,000. A large apartment with sea views can range from R$1,000,000 to R$1,500,000. A large four bedroom apartment measuring 410 square metres can range between R$1,300,000 and R$2,200,000.

■ São Conrado has an array of good to luxury houses. A large three bedroom house is available for R$1,000,000. Four bedroom houses start at R$620,000 and five bedroom houses at R$2,800,000.

Botafogo, Flamengo and Urca

The views of Guanabara Bay are quite spectacular; some of the famous landmarks of Brazil can be seen from here and the prices reflect this.

Botafogo is positioned facing Guanabara Bay, shielded from the ocean by Sugar Loaf Mountain and the Urca peninsula. It is a traditional neighbourhood and was once home to former Brazilian President Fernando Henrique Cardoso. The area name, Botafogo, derives from the previous landowner in colonial times, João Pereira de Sousa Botafogo. It is now considered to be a middle- to upper-class neighbourhood with many cinemas, theatres, museums, and an art house cinema as well as two of the largest shopping centres in Rio: Rio Sul and Botafogo Praia Shopping. Botafogo is one of Rio's biggest football teams.

Flamengo is the Portuguese word for Flemish as it is believed that the area was once owned by a Dutchman. It has views of two of Rio's most famous landmarks: the Sugar Loaf Mountain and the statue of Christ the Redeemer. It was once home to embassies in the art deco buildings that abound, but now it is considered to be a solid middle-class neighbourhood. The beachfront is occupied mainly by the Parque do Flamengo which is a park covering over 300 acres.

Urca is considered to be one of the city's safest and most exclusive neighbourhoods. Architecturally it has some of the city's finest buildings and is mainly a low-built area with many traditional houses. Facing part of Guanabara Bay, it is home to the

Sugar Loaf Mountain which marks the end of Guanabara Bay. At the base of the mountain is the cable car which goes up the mountain. It has a small beach, Praia Vermelho, meaning red beach, so named as the sand is red.

Unfortunately for the prospective buyer, little property in this area changes hands; the former house of famous film star and singer Carmen Miranda (*I, I, I, I, think you're great*) is situated here, with a plaque commemorating her residence which is now occupied as a private family home.

Property prices in these areas are very similar.

- One bedroom apartments start at R$156,000.

- Small two bedroom apartments generally are available at R$250,000.

- Large three bedroom apartments typically cost R$560,000 upwards.

- A large seven bedroom house, rarely available in Urca, is for sale for R$2,400,000.

Gavea, Jardim Botanico, Lagoa, Laranjeiras, Cosme Velho, Barra da Tijuca
These form the other desirable areas in the South Zone.

Gavea is an affluent area which attracts mainly the artistic and the intellectual. It is home to what is regarded as the bohemian quarter. Gavea was discovered by the French in 1565 in search of Brazilwood, a timber used for construction of bows for stringed instruments. It has one of the most important universities in the area, PUC – Rio, as well as several schools. It is called Gavea meaning 'top sail' in Portuguese because its highest point at 852 metres resembles the top sail of a sailing ship. It is home to Hipodromo da Gavea, a horse-racing course.

- One bedroom apartments for sale in this area start at R$300,000. Two bedroom apartments start at R$370,000, and three bedroom apartments range from R$420,000 to R$700,000. Four bedroom apartments start at R$450,000.

- Four bedroom houses in the area start at R$1,800,000; five bedroom houses range between R$2,200,000 and R$3,500,000.

- A penthouse apartment starts at R$450,000, with a three bedroom penthouse at R$1,200,000 and a four bedroom penthouse at R$1,750,000.

Jardim Botanico derives its name from the world-famous botanical garden located in the area which was founded by John VI of Portugal in 1808. It is a very exclusive area of the city and attracts many celebrities who have large mansions in the area, probably because there are no *favelas* there.

- Two bedroom apartments start at R$420,000 and three bedroom apartments range from R$790,000 to R$1,800,000. Four bedroom apartments start at R$1,000,000.

- Four bedroom houses start at R$1,200,000; five bedroom houses start at R$1,600,000.

The Lagoa neighbourhood is centred around the Rodrigo de Freitas lagoon.

- A small, one bedroom apartment starts at R$190,000; two bedroom apartments range from R$370,000 to R$400,000; three bedroom apartments range from R$470,000 to R$1,800,000; four bedroom apartments range from R$1,300,000 to R$3,200,000.

- Houses in the area start at R$1,800,000 for a four bedroom house.

- Two bedroom penthouses start at R$1,000,000.

Laranjeiras and Cosme Velho are two of the city's oldest areas and can trace historical buildings back to the 17th century when there were sumptuous country houses in the area. Laranjeiras neighbours the Corcovado Mountain which sports the statue of Christ the Redeemer. Cosme Velho is at the beginning of the Corcovado Mountain and is a very popular tourist attraction as it has the train track winding its way up the Corcovado Mountain to the statue at the 700-metre peak. The statue itself stands 39.6 metres above that. The train ride is not to be ventured by the faint hearted, but it is possible to drive to the summit by car. Either way, it is a perilous journey.

■ Apartments in these areas are rare, but a five bedroom house starts at just below R$1,000,000.

Barra da Tijuca is a newer, less well-known neighbourhood, but it has some of the most expensive real estate in Brazil. *Barra* means 'port' or 'sandbank' and *Tijuca* means 'swamp' in Tupi Indian language. It doesn't live up to its name now and resembles a concrete jungle with its high-rise buildings. It is located in the west zone of the city (*Zona Oeste*). There are 18km of beach, much of which is polluted, three main lakes and some smaller ones. From Barra da Tijuca it is possible to have views of the mountains, the sea and the lakes and the price of properties reflect the views.

Although a quiet neighbourhood originally, in the 1980s there was a population explosion and it now mirrors an American neighbourhood with its apartment blocks and town houses, supermarkets, shopping malls and entertainment centres. It has the biggest shopping mall: Barra Shopping as well as the New York City Centre, Barra Square and Barra Point which are all also shopping malls. Cinemas and restaurants are located inside the malls. Unfortunately with the population explosion came the *favelas*, which don't prevent real estate in the area being some of the most expensive in Brazil.

■ The starting price of a one bedroom apartment measuring 90 square metres is R$210,000. Two bedroom apartments range from R$230,000 to R$1,250,000, depending on the size and view. Three bedroom apartments range from R$390,000 to R$1,500,000.

■ If you're after a house in Barra da Tijuca you can look to pay a minimum of R$1,300,000 for a house measuring 567 square metres going up to R$4,250,000 for a house on a plot of 1,000 square metres.

■ Three bedroom penthouses come with a price tag of over R$1,000,000; for a four bedroom penthouse the range is between R$1,900,000 and R$3,000,000.

There are many websites which deal in central Rio properties, some of which are more specialised such as www.rioapartments.com and www.judicearaujo.com.br that sell anything from a one bedroom flat to a seven bedroom mansion, and everything else in between.

Other Cities in the State of Rio de Janeiro
Cidade Niteroi

Niteroi is the only Brazilian city to have been founded by a Tupi Indian – called Arariboia in 1573. It is a city across the bay, approximately 13km from Rio de Janeiro, and can be reached either by road over the Niteroi-Rio bridge which takes about an hour to cross from Rio (being one of the longest bridges in the world), by hydrofoil which takes about 12 minutes or by the ferry which takes about 20 minutes.

Perhaps the most famous landmark in the city is the Niteroi Contemporary Art Museum, homage to Brazilian modernist architecture by Oscar Niemeyer.

This is a commuter city for people working in Rio and property prices are a lot cheaper than Rio de Janeiro *and* it overlooks Rio.

■ Typically, a large three bedroom house in a 1200 square metres plot is available from R$495,000. For more details see www.virtuaimoveis.com.br.

West of Rio State
Cidade Parati

Parati is rich in nature, history and culture. It is located between Rio de Janeiro and São Paulo and is 232km south of Rio de Janeiro. There is a small airfield for helicopters and light aircraft.

The historic centre is subject to National Trust regulations, with a large portion of the city being located in the Bocaina mountain range. There is also the sea at Parati Bay whose coastline is preserved. The city is very old and was founded in 1667 around the church of Nossas Senhora Dos Remedios, the patron saint of the city. It was once of great economic importance owing to sugar cane and the export of gold and precious stones, but numerous pirate attacks stopped the trade. Later in the 20th century its economic power was redeveloped from the tourist trade.

The waters of Parati Bay are some of the most beautiful in Brazil. It is part of the Ilha Grande Bay and has calm and clear waters ideal for diving and sailing. Parati is said to be the Brazilian diving capital and there are diving schools in the area. There are several marinas offering all ancillary services.

Property for sale in Parati is unusual and expensive. Properties in the historical centre, part of a heritage site, can be found in abundance on www.acparaty.com.br: there are even several islands for sale.

■ A 20 hectare island with a five bedroom mansion is for sale for US$1.5m.

■ For the smaller investor, a 26 bedroom hotel is for sale for US$1m.

■ Alternatively if you like to live and work from home, a two storey building is for sale for US$250,000 with residential accommodation on the top floor and a business on the ground floor. See also www.glo-con.com.

Cidade Angra dos Reis

The name means the 'King's harbour' and includes 365 islands and 2,000 beaches in the west of Rio State.

Angra dos Reis lies between Rio de Janeiro and São Paolo states and is accessed via the BR 101 RIO-Santos highway. It is approximately 133km south of Rio de Janeiro. There is an airfield for light planes and, if arriving by boat, there are yacht clubs and a marina in the city.

This part of the Costa Verde Fluminense is best explored by boat. The biggest island is Isla Grande and on it can be found numerous trails, beaches and waterfalls. In the past it even hosted a prison for over 60 years. It was one of the most important ports in the state and imported not only goods, but also slaves. Amazingly, this area is also the controversial site of Brazilian nuclear power plants.

The beach sand here is very fine and waters are clear and calm. Places to visit include Praia Grande, Praia do Retiro and the navy school. There is also Ilha do Gipoia which translated means 'Snake Island' as it resembles the shape of a snake. There are different types of beaches including surfing beaches: Grande and Feras, whereas Praia da Piedade is a family beach. There are also shipwrecks to be explored at Maciel. There are waterfalls at Serra do Mar. Some of the strongest waves are to be found at Praia Brava while those looking for solitude can find it at Praia Secreta. Nearby is Mambucaba, an ancient village for those interested in exploring the history of the islands, including several historic buildings rich in architecture dating from the 18th century, such as the Mansao do Morcego, meaning 'Bat Mansion' once owned by the pirate Juan de Lorenzo in the 19th century. Hotel do Frade and golf resort offers excellent accommodation and entertainment while deciding whether to buy in this locality.

It is something of a playground for the rich and famous. However, you can buy a very reasonably priced property here, depending on closeness to the beach front.

■ At the upper end of the market, R$400,000 will provide a four bedroom house in a condominium; R$600,000 a larger four bedroom house in a condo; R$750,000 a four bedroom house not in a condo; R$950,000 a large house in a plot of 6,200; R$1,500,000 a four bedroom house with all rooms facing the sea, in a condo; R$2,000,000 a beachfront house not in a condo on a plot of 15,000 square metres with a private beach; R$2,500,000 a three bedroom house in a condo in a plot of 1,280 square metres; for R$4,000,000 a four bedroom house in a condo on a plot of 1,800,000 square metres. See further www.judicearaujo.com.br.

■ At the middle to lower end of the market, a three bedroom villa in a condominium here, say, 50 metres to the beachfront with a pool will cost you US$145,000. A three bedroom apartment with a sea view typically costs US$65,000. A four bedroom villa with a sea view will cost about US $120,000 and a five bedroom house with a sea view and a pool about US$150,000. Although renowned for its crystal clear waters and coastal scenery, it has *favelas* as well as a nuclear power station in the vicinity. See www.onlinepropertyworld. com.

North of Rio State
Petrópolis
The city of Petrópolis is in the hills to the north of Rio de Janeiro and cool – in both senses. It is located approximately 70km north of Rio de Janeiro. There are reasonably priced guest houses and more expensive hotels to stay at when deciding whether to invest in Petrópolis.

Rua Teresa, is the main shopping street in historical Petrópolis selling clothing and accessories. Approximately 10km from historic Petrópolis is the district of Bingen where the price of goods is cheaper than in Centro and where there is a wider variety of shops, including furniture shops. Itaipava is 15km from central Petrópolis and has excellent restaurants as well as antique and arts and crafts shops amongst other more upmarket outlets selling fashion items to furniture.

■ A price tag of R$250,000 includes a house with three bedrooms on one level, in a condominium, with a land area of 2,500 square metres. A three bedroom house in a condo can be purchased for R$590,000 in a larger plot of 2,700 square metres; a four bedroom house is available for R$750,000 in a plot of 2,800 square metres.

■ For R$1,000,000 you can buy a five bedroom house in a condo; for more than five bedrooms expect to pay over R$1,500,000 in a 4,800 square metre plot.

■ A large house on a plot of 16,800 square metres will cost R$2,000,000.

■ R$2,500,000 buys a very large house with 13 bedrooms, each with en suite facilities, on a plot of 15,000 square metres.

■ R$3,500,000 will buy a very large house in the noblest area of Itaipava, on a plot of 68,000 square metres. See www.judicearaujo.com.br.

East of Rio State
Regiao de Lagoa
This area lies towards the east of Rio State and is called the 'Region of the lakes' (in fact, magnificent sea-fed lagoons), where there are no *favelas* and no power plants. The region includes the cities: Marica, Ponta Negra, Saquarema, Araruama, Arrial do Cabo, Cabo Frio, up as far as Búzios. You can take the scenic route along the coast or you can go on what passes hereabouts for a toll motorway.

Marica and Ponta Negra
Marica is the closest town to Rio city after Niteroi, although not very developed in terms of facilities and can be reached within an hour from Rio Centro. Despite its close proximity to Rio, it is a sleepy town which may experience rapid growth

as there has recently been a lot of international investment in the area with the building of condominiums. It is currently an ideal location for those who shun crowds and like miles of beach to themselves.

Neighbouring Ponta Negra is even less developed.

■ A two to three bedroom house ranges from R$165,000 to R$435,000.

■ A four bedroom, four bathroom, house ranges from R$189,000 to R$280,000 and a five bedroom, four to five bathroom house ranges from R$420,000 to just under R$1,000,000. See further www.riowild.com.

Saquarema

Saquarema is famous for hosting the world surfing championships in Itauna and the national volleyball championships in the arenas at Barra Nova. It also provides the setting for a popular TV soap *Luz do Sol*, with its stereotypical goodies and baddies all aided and abetted by scheming domestic staff.

Saquarema is a charming, seaside city inhabited mainly by Cariocas (natives of Rio) who bring up their families in this area away from the hustle and bustle of Rio Centro. It is a family-orientated area and lacks the usual facilities that a young single person would be looking for, such as a bustling nightlife. Despite this, the place livens up at the weekends when the families get together and have their usual *churrascaria* (barbecue), and a spot of sunbathing on the endless stretches of beach. Although it lacks fine international cuisine, what it does have is plentiful Brazilian barbecued fish and meat, served up at the many kiosks that line the beaches. Usually, the weekend comes alive on Friday and Saturday nights when the families, including every generation from great grandparent to great grandchild go to town and have a pizza at the town square. Lakes Shopping area is also popular, and from Thursdays to the end of the weekend, you can find live Brazilian music here. Anyone thinking of coming to visit the area before buying can stay at any one of an array of *pousadas* (inns), the best of which, in terms of facilities, is the Maasai Hotel and Club in Itauna (tel +55 22 2651 1092).

Apart from the physical beauty of the place, this town can claim 40km of beach front, broken only by the rock on which stands the Nossa Senhora de Nazareth Church lit up by blue lasers hidden in the rock to make it appear as if the church is floating on the water. The local *prefeitura* has been making visible improvements, and there is now a large new tourist office where they speak many languages (tel +55 22 2651 2123).

If you are looking for a beach-front property or a small farm, this might well be the place to buy it. There are many estate agents in the town, as well as some selling property over the internet.

The area of Saquarema is primarily sea front on one side and lagoon fronted on the other with roads in between. One of the most spectacular views of Saquarema is seen from the highest point in Saquarema, Morro do Cruz offering a panorama of sea, lagoon and mountain range.

The 20km road along the ocean front is divided into several areas of Saquarema overlooking the ocean, beginning with the first area nearest to the main road to Rio you will find Jacone, Barra Nova, Boqueirao, Gravata, Centro and, finally, Itauna.

Jacone has a feel of a village and as one would expect, everyone knows everyone else's name. It has one of the largest lagoons in Saquarema with a spectacular mountain backdrop. The road to Rio is through the mountain range unless you don't mind driving along the dirt road for part of the distance to Ponta Negra. There are plans to upgrade this dirt road in the near future and, if this happens, the area will become accessible for daily commuting into Rio Centro.

■ Two bedroom houses are typically available for around R$120,000.

■ Three bedroom houses from R$170,000 upwards on a 450 square metre plot, or if you prefer to build your own, a plot of beachfront land of 450 square metres is available at R$35,000.

Barra Nova is where the picturesque volleyball stadium is located with its own volleyball courts, tennis courts, football pitch, restaurants and accommodation. There are also many *pousadas* accommodating the influx during the championships.

■ Typically, a three bedroom house on the beach-front can be bought for R$145,000.

Boqueirao also has a village feel to it, especially so with the road on the lagoon.

■ A three bedroom house on the lagoon on a 450 square metre plot in this area costs around R$160,000, and a similar plot with a larger house on the ocean front costs over R$250,000.

Gravata is a perfect distance from Centro with its kiosks and shopping giving it a peaceful atmosphere and yet it is within a few minutes of Centro. This is another much sought-after area in Saquarema and the houses along the ocean and lagoon front are much in demand.

■ Lagoon-front houses range from R$160,000 to R$300,000 and ocean-front houses range from R$350,000 to R$750,000.

■ A building plot on the ocean front can be bought for R$70,000.

Itauna is regarded as one of the best areas of Saquarema and has apartment blocks, houses, mansions, condominiums and, importantly, a safe part of the beach for children to practise swimming and surfing.

■ A typical two bedroom apartment with ocean views, costs R$148,000.

■ A two bedroom house in a condominium ranges from R$130,000 to R$180,000.

■ A three bedroom house in a condominium ranges from R$160,000 to R$260,000.

■ Outside the condominiums, a small one storey, two bedroom house on a large plot of 1,250 square metres directly on the beach costs R$500,000.

■ A three/four bedroom house, directly on the beach, in a 1,200 square metre plot, fetches over R$650,000.

Morro do Cruz is the highest point in Saquarema and has spectacular views of the ocean, lagoon and mountains and the prices reflect this.

- The cost of a four bedroom house in a condominium starts at R$370,000, including shared leisure facilities with 19 other houses and the usual security features.

Sampaio Correia is on the road to Rio and is where the mountains touch the sky. There are many small farms here.

- A fruit 'farm' on 15,000 square metres costs R$250,000 including a three bedroom house, swimming pool, barbecue area, a football field and its own mineral water well.

- A smaller 'farm' of 6,250 square metres costs R$100,000, including a three bedroom house.

For more properties in the region of the lakes area visit www.virtuaimoveis.com.br.

Arraial do Cabo

The city is located about 140km east of Rio de Janeiro Centro, between Búzios and Cabo Frio, on one side, and Saquarema and Araruama on the other. At Arraial do Cabo, there are white sand beaches with crystal clear waters, sand dunes, visible shoals of fish, ecological reservations and one of the world's most rewarding locations for fishing. It is a very popular destination for those seeking natural beauty in simple and relatively unspoilt settings. Arraial was originally a fishing village known as 'Atlantic Paradise' by its local inhabitants, offering lagoons, beaches, reefs and sand dunes. One of its most attractive lagoons is called Lagoa Azul ('Blue Lagoon'), which is a very popular destination.

There are several beaches, each offering their own special attractions: Pontal Beach is very popular with those wishing to undertake serious fishing and Prainha ('Little Beach') is 1km long and has lots of kiosks and low buildings. Praia Grande ('Big or Long Beach'), 1.3km in length, also offers simple fresh cuisine at the many beach kiosks.

- A loft apartment with fantastic sea views is available at R$120,000. See further: www.virtuaimoveis.com.br.

See www.lagoservice.com.br for more properties in the area.

Cidade Cabo Frio

The city of Cabo Frio has an appeal for the young and upwardly mobile with its clear blue water, which is very cold; powdery white sand dunes, restaurants and clubs. It has a good infrastructure to cater for its international visitors with its own international airport, which is also the nearest airport to its even more fashionable neighbour, Armação de Búzios.

■ A two bedroom apartment with ocean views costs around R$245,000.

■ A three bedroom, four bathroom, ocean-front house costs in excess of R$270,000 and a four bedroom, six bathroom house costs more than R$615,000.

For more properties in this area see www.virtuaimoveis.com.br, www.lagoservice. com.br and www.riowild.com.

Cidade Armação de Búzios

Known simply as Búzios, the city began as a small fishing village, visited by pirates and slave traffickers. The area is situated on an isthmus with more than 20 beaches together with a developed infrastructure, including good international cuisine, excellent shops and a vibrant nightlife. The popularity of the area as an international destination came with a short visit from Brigitte Bardot in the 1960s.

Búzios has been rated by various travel articles as one of the top ten holiday destinations in the world, as well as one of the most beautiful. It is 30 minutes by road to Cabo Frio international airport and two hours by road to Rio de Janeiro.

The main attractions of the area are its many and varied beaches.

■ João Fernandinho Beach is a relatively small beach with calm waters, which has as one of its attractions many purveyors of a wide variety of sea food.

■ Brava Beach has strong waves for surf lovers as well as those who like to bathe in the nude.

Trancoso, Bahia

The historic city of Pelourinho, Salvador, Bahia

Natural pools amongst the sand dunes at Canoa Quebrada, Ceara

Riding the waves on the Foz do Iguacu, Parana

Historic part of Florianopolis, Santa Catarina

Floating in the River Formoso, Bonito, Mato Grosso do Sul

Ponta Verde Beach, Maceio, Alagoas

The Blue Lagoon, Jericoacoara, Ceara

Historic houses in the city of Olinda, Pernambuco

Coconut Palms fronting the lagoon, Maceio, Alagoas

Cajus – the fruit and nut cashew

Beira-Mar, Fortaleza, Ceara

A young Amazonian boy climbing the wonderous Acai berry tree in Macapa, Amapa

■ Tartaruga Beach, also known as Turtle Beach, as the turtles lay their eggs there, has calm, warm waters and many places to eat. It is also popular with divers.

■ Geriba Beach is popular with the so-called beautiful people who like to sun bathe Brazilian style; standing and posing. Those wishing to explore the isthmus will find part of the trail leading to Ferradurinha Beach nearby.

■ Ferradura Beach has calm, clear waters, although not warm. It is a popular and safe place for sailing.

Besides the beaches there is the Búzios Golf Club, with a world-class, 18-hole course, considered one of the best in Latin America. There is ample opportunity for diving and the city also hosts international sailing competitions. Rua das Pedras is the main shopping street and it has an array of bars, shops, restaurants, art galleries and a cinema. It lives up to its name because it is indeed a roughly cobbled street. Búzios isn't just about the beach and shopping. For the eco-lover, there are the Emerências and Taua Reserves with over 300 butterfly and 60 bird species.

Búzios is a wonderful place, without any desire for high-rise hotels. Those visiting before buying a property can stay at any number of *pousadas* and hotels. Pousada Buziana offers reasonably priced accommodation and is located at Tartaruga Beach; for more details see www.buzianatour.com. More expensive accommodation can be found in Búzios Centro, such as Hotel Mandragora; for further details see www.buziosmandragora.com.

■ A big house on a plot of 1,000 square metres, with a built area of 700 square metres (over three floors) on Ferradura Beach (one of the most exclusive areas), will set you back US$2,500,000. In this sort of area, prices are much more aligned to the purchasing power of the foreign investor. Such a house would have six master suites, two family bathrooms, three reception rooms, barbecue area, garaging for five cars, swimming pool, boat shed and housekeeper's quarters. This beach boasts calm, crystal clear waters all year round.

■ With a smaller budget, a much smaller, five bedroom house in the same area will cost US$250,000.

■ At the lower end of the scale you can pay US$150,000 for a three bedroom house in a condominium, away from the beach in Centro, where there are all the shops and restaurants. The size of the land would be about 200 square metres.

■ However, going up to a four bedroom house on a plot of 250 square metres in such a condominium would take you up to US$250,000. See, for example: www.alexanderrichards.co.uk, www.propertyline.co.uk, www.judicearaujo. com.br.

The State of São Paulo

São Paulo is the second largest city in the world, after Mexico City, with a population of roughly 20 million people. It is an industrial and commercial centre and not an especially beautiful place.

There has been a change in the city's economic profile in the last ten years, away from a purely industrial base towards commercial and service industries. Intensive manpower has been replaced by a great number of high tech companies and service providers including law, investment banking, information technology, advertising, consultancy and radio and TV. In the last few years, São Paulo has become host to a number of international events including leather goods and textiles fairs, international construction and cosmetics fairs, services and apartments fairs, automobile and book fairs.

■ Depending on your budget, you can buy an apartment in São Paulo for US$230,000, 40 minutes from the international airport, 15 minutes from a domestic airport and in walking distance of two mainline train stations; the block offers its own pool, gym, garage, playground and gardens – the apartment being 220 square metres.

■ For those going slightly further afield, there are investment opportunities at around US$150,000 which buys 49,000 square metres, with a four bedroom house and three separate houses, suitable for letting or as a bed and breakfast, with a shared pool, basket ball and soccer pitches, available through www.overseasrealestate.co.uk.

■ For those interested in an ocean-front luxury villa, the area Ubatuba offers a five bedroom, eight bathroom luxury house with its own heated pool, for just less than US$1.2m.

THE NORTH EAST

The coastal states of interest in the North East of Brazil include Bahia, Alagoas, Pernambuco, Paraíba, Rio Grande do Norte and Ceará.

The State of Bahia

The state of Bahia is north east of Rio de Janeiro State. The temperatures are high all the year round and the rainy season is between June and August.

Salvador

Salvador is the capital of Bahia and has a large international airport as well as domestic access from all the states of Brazil. Many cruise ships also stop in Salvador.

Salvador has the full infrastructure of a modern city. The old town of Salvador has some wonderful historic buildings and is a major tourist attraction, although some parts are very industrialised, being home to a number of car manufacturers.

Once a principal port for the importation of slaves into Brazil, it is no surprise that it still retains an African influence, not just in its music, but also in its food. Spicy fish stew is one of its main dishes, along with shrimp *bobo*. Nevertheless the African influence sits alongside a great variety of mixed cuisine.

The *Carnaval* in Salvador is a big event and operates on the sound truck system introduced in the 1950s. It is not for the timid or the faint-hearted. Until 1950 the *Carnaval* was a low-key celebration held in private clubs, not the street. In Salvador alone there are 70 *Carnaval* blocks! (A *Carnaval* block consists of two trucks with a band playing, and lots of party revellers, some on the trucks and some following, wearing the uniform of that particular block. Anyone can take part by joining in the procession on payment of a small fee.)

The Coastline of Salvador is one of the longest in Brazil and stretches over 50km. The various beaches have diversity in terms of flora and fauna and some are calm and ideal for diving and fishing whilst others with stronger waves are sought after by surfers.

Recently, Bahia has attracted large-scale investment. It is not uncommon to see almost back-to-back resorts and condominiums, offering some golf, sailing, fishing, diving, riding, trekking, etc. They also have their own shops, bank and medical services.

■ Typically, a condominium flat costs US$150,000.

■ A house on a large plot of over 2,500 square metres, would cost between US$1–1.5m.

Property advertised for sale in Salvador at the time of writing included:

■ A three bedroom house in Salvador 50 metres to the beach costs R$190,000.

■ Houses priced from R$350,000 can be built on a lagoon in a condominium with a private club, tennis courts, a large swimming pool, kids' club, sauna, fitness centre and water sports facilities.

■ A five bedroom, three bathroom house with ocean and sand dune views near to a PGA golf course on a plot of over 1,000 square metres costs R$420,000.

■ A three bedroom house with a constructed area of 574 square metres in a plot of 784 square metres, costs R$480,000 comes with its own swimming pool and gardens.

■ A house for a millionaire's lifestyle on a 20,000 square metre plot including a five bedroom, five bathroom house with the possibility of an artist's studio and guest house as an extra, has an initial asking price of R$700,000.

■ A 'wow factor' house with five bedrooms, five bathrooms, on a 5,000 square metre plot overlooking the lagoon, with a home cinema and two maids' quarters is available for R$2,500,000.

■ An historic house in Centro used as a hotel offering first class accommodation is priced at around R$4,000,000.

For more information on these, see www.alexanderrichards.co.uk. Below is a selection of properties available on www.propertybond.co.uk.

- A one bedroom apartment for R$99,000 in a condominium with a gym, pool, spa and restaurants, away from the beachfront. A similar apartment on the beach-front costs over R$180,000.

- A one bedroom apartment on the beach-front would typically cost R$180,000.

- Away from the condominiums, a three bedroom flat not on the beach-front costs R$190,000;

- A small farm of ten hectares in Salvador can be purchased for around R$190,000.

- A cashew farm of 28 hectares is priced at R$300,000.

- A small, nine bedroom hotel (*pousada*) can be bought for R$550,000 in grounds of 1,200 square metres.

Praia do Forte

This is a popular area for ecological tourists; it is family orientated, offering decent dining and shopping, but not much in the way of entertainment. It is favoured as a middle-class holiday destination.

- Luxury, beachfront, three bedroom, three bathroom, air-conditioned apartments are available for R$695,000 in a beach front condominium.

- Overlooking the lagoon at Praia do Forte is a three bedroom house on a 1,100 square metre plot with its own jetty for R$750,000.

- In the village, close to the beach, there is a four bedroom, four bathroom house in a plot of over 1,000 square metres available in a closed condominium for R$850,000. It includes a swimming pool.

■ There are also investment opportunities available, such as an eight bedroom *pousada* for R$1,200,000.

■ A small apartment hotel with 15 apartments is for sale in the village near to the beach for R$1,800,000, possibly with existing contracts for European tour operators.

For further details of the above opportunities see www.alexanderrichards.co.uk.

Costa do Sauípe

This is about 65km from the Luis Eduardo Magalhaes International airport. It was established as a major tourist destination at the beginning of this century with the opening of five 5-star hotels: a Marriott, two Sofitels, a Breezes Superclub and a Renaissance. There is also a PGA golf course. This stretch of the beach offers a combination of sand dunes and lagoons beyond.

Away from the resorts, Vila Nova da Praia has many handicrafts for sale and holds music concerts and dancing events. For everyday entertainment, it offers many bars and restaurants in the way of pavement cafés.

This is considered to be one of the most beautiful areas of Bahia, with several different landscapes and a lot of wildlife, including whales and rare birds.

Trancoso is some 40 minutes from the ferry which joins Porto Seguro and the airport. This is considered a quiet, exclusive area and a hideaway for the rich and famous.

■ The prices here are high and a metre of beach-front land can cost up to R$20,000.

■ If you are not part of the jet set, you can buy an ordinary village house for around R$200,000.

Arraial d'Ajuda

This can be reached within ten minutes by ferry from the airport. Arraial d'Ajuda lacks the infrastructure of nearby Porto Seguro but provides accommodation for the more discerning. It has traditional Portuguese houses, a golf course, plus good shopping facilities and restaurants. Arraial d'Ajuda attracts rich Brazilians and is fast becoming an international destination.

Porto Seguro

This is one of Brazil's oldest tourist destinations, with many small hotels and nice beaches, stretching along 90km of coastline with coral reefs, bays and Atlantic forests. It has a very lively nightlife and shops stay open through the night. There is a variety of restaurants: French, Italian, Japanese and the *lanchonetes*, or snack bars, offering Brazilian food for sale by the kilo.

The weather is not always dry and warm as it does have a rainy season from May to August. Porto Seguro attracts many foreign tourists and has an international airport.

Some of the best beaches include:

- Muta Beach, which is very popular as it offers very calm and transparent, warm waters which are good for bathing and water sports.

- Taperapua Beach is also another popular beach.

- Mumdai Beach is popular with divers and sportspeople.

- Lagoa Azul Beach has clear seas and big waves.

- Coqueros Beach has golden sand and green seas which attract not just bathers and divers, but also fishermen.

For those wanting a little gentle sport, there is the Terravista golf links.

This area is generally considered to be the middle to end of the housing market.

- A two bedroom flat can be bought for just over R$136,000 in a condominium, with two garage spaces and a shared swimming pool and barbecue. The condominium is 800 metres from the beach, which is famous for its parties.

- If a house is what you are after in a condominium, these are available at R$308,000 for a three bedroom country house at the Xurupita resort, although the villas in the same condominium are more expensive. They have ocean views and large verandas and share leisure facilities such as the pool and other sports facilities.

- Outside the condominium, 100 metres to the beach at Santa Cruz de Cabralia, a five bedroom, five bathroom house on a large plot of 1,695 square metres with a swimming pool is available for R$390,000.

- For a slightly larger budget, at R$430,000, a large ocean-front, modern, three bedroom house is available, with 329 square metres of construction and on a plot of 1,000 square metres with its own swimming pool, sauna, separate maid's house and barbecue area.

- A newly constructed house, 1km from the beach, with four bedrooms and four bathrooms, a swimming pool with a wooden deck and an American style kitchen is available for R$510,000.

- If space is what you're after, R$601,000 will buy 6,300 square metres in front of the beach, with a modern four bedroom house, swimming pool and a lush tropical garden with many fruit trees.

- Investment opportunities exist in the hotel industry. For R$650,000 a 14 apartment hotel is available on a plot of 5,000 square metres, 200 metres from the beach. For R$1,700,000, a hotel with 26 suites is available in central Porto Seguro. There are also opportunities to purchase land for development.

For more information on the above properties see www.alexanderrichards.co.uk.

Maraú

Maraú has been made famous by the author of *The Little Prince*, Antoine de Saint-Exupery, who lived there. There are several buildings dating from the 18th century in the colonial style. It is 469km from Salvador. The only way to reach it is by road and motor boat.

■ Property for sale in Maraú includes a ten-apartment beach-front *pousada* with 40 metres of beach front on a 6,000 square metre plot, including a restaurant, internet access and telephone for R$1,200,000.

Itacare and Ilhéus

These are on the Cacao coast, 440km south of Salvador, and the closest national airport is Ilhéus; the closest International airport is Salvador. There are restaurants, inns and hotels but, as yet, the infrastructure is inadequate to cope with a great influx of visitors. There are beaches and hills and the best ones near the town centre do have some tourist facilities.

Resende Beach is near the town in a protected area and has no construction. The best beach with infrastructure is the Concah Beach. Tiriraca is a beach for surfers.

■ Only a five minute walk to the beach at Ilhéus, a three storey house with five bedrooms, three en suites with ocean views, three reception rooms, swimming pool, maid's accommodation and solar heating is available at R$700,000.

■ Property for sale in Itacare includes an investment opportunity of an eight bedroom *pousada*, a separate two bedroom house and a gift shop for just under R$620,000.

■ For eco lovers there is an eco resort and condominium properties for sale located in what was previously a cocoa farm, preserving the essential natural flora and fauna. Prices start at R$700,000 for a two bedroom bungalow with sea views. There are many facilities available in the resort such as a hotel, 24-hour security and the usual utilities.

■ There are also plots of land for sale for the self-build enthusiast, starting at just over R$409,700.

■ There are houses for sale in a smaller condominium of only 11 houses, with shared leisure facilities such as a pool, barbecue area and sports facilities, with prices starting at R$330,000 for a two bedroom villa.

For more ideas, see www.alexanderrichards.co.uk.

The State of Alagoas

Maceió

Maceió is the capital of the state Alagoas, and has its origins in sugar cane, leather, tobacco, coconut and spice exports in the 18th century. It became the state capital on December 9th 1839.

Maceió has a good tourist infrastructure and the beach areas are divided into town beaches, such as Pajucara, Ponta Verde, and Jatiuca, which is very lively, especially so when there is live music. Out of town, to the north where the beaches are much quieter there is an abundance of coconut trees, rivers and quiet bars. There is also Croa Island which is even more peaceful, with rustic bars and peaceful areas. The south seashore has beaches such as Frances and Gunga Beaches, which have natural lagoon pools offering surfing and other water sports.

Maceió airport receives flights from all national states and attracts some international airlines.

- Building plots near to the beach measuring 450 square metres are available to a developer for R$60,000.

- Another developer is offering similar-sized plots in a condominium for R$70,000.

- A nine bedroom *pousada* on a 1,600 square metre plot two blocks from the beach is for sale at R$500,000.

- In Maceió itself, starting at R$801,000 are beach-front lots. The development includes a variety of leisure facilities including tennis courts, squash courts, volleyball, a bar, gym, a club, a cycle lane as well as 24-hour security.

For more details see www.alexanderrichards.co.uk.

The State of Ceará

Fortaleza

Fotaleza has a warm and dry tropical climate, with average annual temperatures of around 27°C and it offers warm bathing waters. There is a complete infrastructure, including a vibrant nightlife. This means that it is noisy – the Brazilians love their music and generally making a noise. There are also museums, churches, theatres and historical buildings.

The airport is near to the city, and it provides domestic and international connections.

Iracema, Meireles and Futuro Beaches are some of the more popular ones. There are walks on the famous Beira Mar Avenue Promenade. The city offers boat trips and has recently started to attract businesses holding conferences and international events.

There is a large open-air shopping mall at Monsenhor Tabosa Street.

Because of all these attractions, Ceará has become a major site for developers.

- For those wishing to purchase a sea view apartment in a beach-front condominium with a pool, gym and sauna, for retirement or holidays, a small, one bedroom apartment of 51 square metres costs R$100,000.

- A two bedroom apartment would cost about R$160,000. This development is about an hour from the airport.

- Many developers are offering off-plan properties and some developers faced with increasing competition are offering a cash discount of 5% off the purchase price. A R$4,000 deposit will secure the property; with the remainder of the purchase price to be paid in 24 monthly instalments.

- Some big developers are offering not just to sell property but packages which include management and rental of the property. Typically a one bedroom flat could be let for R$100-180 per day. Another service which such developers offer is legal assistance at a fixed cost. These condominiums are popular with Europeans. As a result, European return flights to Fortaleza can cost as little as between US$600-1,000 and a flight from a central European destination to Fortaleza takes around seven hours.

■ There are many new and re-sale properties available away from the resorts. These represent excellent value for money. Plots of land are also cheap.

■ A large plot of land measuring 2,391 square metres near the sea can be bought for R$105,000.

■ A plot of over 5,000 square metres, a short walk from the beach can be bought for R$90,000. This would be large enough to build a *pousada*.

New and resale properties represent excellent investment potential.

■ A three bedroom apartment in a high-rise block is available at R$120,000.

■ Four bedroom, each with en suite bathroom, open plan villas with a swimming pool start from R$180,000 with sea views from the first floor in a 1,050 square metre plot.

■ A five bedroom villa, 200 metres from the beach can be bought for R$180,000 with a small pool.

■ A beach bar on Praia do Futuro is available for R$200,000.

■ A four bedroom villa on a large plot of 900 square metres in Fortaleza can be bought for R$210,000, with its own swimming pool and soccer pitch surrounded by coconut trees.

■ A four bedroom villa in a fine neighbourhood can be bought for R$245,000 including a swimming pool and two detached caretakers' houses, only 7km from the airport.

■ A four bedroom apartment in a block with 24-hour security and shared leisure facilities in Meireles, one of Fortaleza's best neighbourhoods, can be bought for R$250,000. For the same price, 31km out of Fortaleza to Icarai, a six bedroom villa, with separate maid's accommodation and a separate caretaker's house with a swimming pool, multi sports court and barbecue is available.

■ If you want to escape the hustle and bustle of the modern city then a four bedroom beach-front villa in a tranquil setting approximately 80km outside of Fortaleza at Aguas Belas, can be bought for R$250,000, including separate caretaker's accommodation, barbecue area and garage for two cars.

■ If you have to be by the sea, at Praia do Combuco a five bedroom villa with sea views, sunsets and sand dunes is available at R$250,000.

■ In Morro Branco, a peaceful and tranquil area, a three bedroom villa on a large plot of 1,350 square metres can be bought for R$265,000, including separate maid's accommodation and caretaker's house, a swimming pool, barbecue deck and double garage.

■ In Meireles, a large, three bedroom apartment can be bought in a large block for R$290,000.

■ An investment opportunity for R$295,000 exists on a plot of 1,000 square metres in Praia do Futuro, Fortaleza with a modern structure that could be used for a number of commercial purposes such a restaurant, bar, nightclub or gym (a way of life in Brazil).

■ In Agua Belas is a large, four bedroom, four bathroom, single-storey villa on a plot of over 4,000 square metres on the ocean front with a pool for R$298,000.

■ At Guajiru Beach a fantastic villa with its own soccer pitch in a plot of 1,144 square metres is available at R$300,000 with enough space to build another villa.

■ For the larger family there is a nine bedroom villa available with swimming pool, barbecue area and garage for four cars at R$320,000 approximately 35km outside of Fortaleza.

■ A six bedroom *pousada* is available for R$346,500, 19km from Fortaleza and the airport.

■ A large penthouse apartment of 586 square metres is available on two floors in Praia do Futuro with four bedrooms, a separate guest apartment and separate maid's accommodation for R$380,000.

■ A twenty room beach-front hotel is available at R$400,000, 56km from down town Fortaleza.

■ A large modern and stylish three bedroom apartment is available in a secure block with shared leisure facilities in the Meireles neighbourhood of Fortaleza for R$420,000.

■ A new, large, four bedroom apartment with an internal space of 274 square metres is available in the heart of Fortaleza in Guararapes. It has shared leisure facilities and is priced at R$474,000.

■ A few minutes from Fortaleza is a three bedroom, two storey villa in a plot of over 600 square metres for R$510,000.

■ A small farm in the São Goncalo area consisting of 44,000 square metres, including a five bedroom main house, a three bedroom caretaker's cottage, a two bedroom staff cottage, stables, a pond, lake, paddocks, 2,300 fruit trees and marmalade-making equipment, 300 sheep and grass fields, is available for R$525,000.

■ Several large three bedroom apartments are available in a new block, with two apartments per floor, in the Mucuripe area of central Fortaleza and are being offered at R$525,776.

■ A 21 acre farm in Pacajus is available for R$550,000.

■ An eight bedroom villa in a good location close to the airport and facilities is available for R$572,000.

■ Within easy reach of Praia do Combuco is a magnificent six bedroom villa in large plot of 1,600 square metres; it has a built area of 500 square metres and is for sale at R$600,000.

■ R$650,00 will buy a large penthouse apartment measuring 620 square metres, with its own swimming pool.

■ A large beach-front guesthouse in a plot of 1,600 square metres with 24 suites is for sale at Praia da Caponga, 56km from Fortaleza down town, for R$900,000.

■ For R$1,000,000, at Iguape Beach, there is a beach-front hotel with 28 rooms; for the same price is a 26 room beach-front hotel at Praia do Futuro beach.

■ A 47 bedroom apartment hotel, at Praia Pacheco, located thirty minutes from Fortaleza International airport, on a cliff top with steps down to the beach, is available for R$1,200,000. For the same price you can buy a huge private villa in a plot of 1,640 square metres with a constructed area of 850 square metres, within a few minutes of the airport, down town and the beach.

■ R$1,200,000 will also buy a huge three bedroom apartment in the exclusive area of Meireles.

■ A four bedroom beach-front apartment is available in an exclusive block at Mucuripe for R$1,345,696 and there are several investment hotel opportunities ranging from R$1,800,000 to R$3,850,000.

Further information about properties for sale in Ceará can be found on www.alexanderrichards.co.uk and www.propertybond.co.uk.

The State of Paraíba

João Pessoa

João Pessoa is the capital of this state. It lies at the most easterly point of Brazil, with an average annual temperature is 26°C.

The modern history of this area dates from when the Portuguese arrived in 1585. It has a rich architectural history in the Baroque style. Besides its historic buildings, it offers warm seas and white sand. The United Nations has declared it the second greenest city in the world (the first is Paris).

Of particular interest are the pool formations, especially at low tide, around the islands of Areia and Vermelho where you may see corals and beautifully coloured fish. They are protected by a sand bank which is a mile long and half a mile wide. This is a very popular tourist destination and has an excellent infrastructure.

It has an international and a national airport and has attracted a great deal of European investment. The Brazil transport ministry will be ploughing R$1.7 billion into the three north easterly states of Paraíba, Pernambuco and Rio Grande do Norte, to increase tourism in these states. Tourism has already increased by 80% over the last three years. Many people who have visited João Pessoa say that it is a very tranquil state capital city.

- There are plots of land available, starting at just below R$30,000, for a 360 square metre plot up to around R$100,000 for a 1,200 square metre plot. These prices reflect the fact that they are 50 metres from the beach and are in an elevated position with sea views.

- There are also off-plan apartments, and for a two bedroom apartment, two minutes from the sea (and with sea views), the price is R$110,000. These properties are near hotels, restaurants, banks, markets, churches and shops.

- A completed two bedroom, two bathroom apartment can be bought for R$159,000, with sea views, on one floor, 70 metres from the sea.

- A similar three bedroom apartment costs just under R$185,000.

- In the country, away from the beach, R$285,000 will buy a three bedroom country house in ten acres. The house comes with a swimming pool, a barbecue area and a caretaker's cottage.

- R$625,000 will buy you ten acres, stables, horse competition and training ground and a large, luxurious main house with a swimming pool, barbecue area, guest house and a property-keeper's cottage, all of which is just 15 minutes' drive from João Pessoa city centre.

■ If you really must be on the beach-front, then R$1,750,000 will buy a luxury villa on the beach in 850 square metres with a large pool and seven bedrooms.

See further: www.propertybond.co.uk.

The State of Pernambuco

This comprises a comparatively narrow coastal zone in the North East of Brazil neighbouring Paraíba. It is hot, with a humid climate, relieved by the south eastern trade winds. The inland region is high, stony and dry. There are hot days and cool nights. There are two main seasons: the dry season and the wet season; the rainy season is from March to June. The climate is mild, because of the Serra das Russas Mountains. Some of the towns are located over a thousand metres above sea level where the temperature can descend to below 5°C in winter.

Recife

The capital, Recife, is Brazil's second largest city. Its port provides a gateway for tourists and the sun shines all year round. The tourist sector is highly developed and it boasts one of the best infrastructures for tourists and business travellers alike. Recife derives from the Portuguese word for reef, which is not surprising as coral reefs line the coast.

One of the most popular areas in the state of Pernambuco is Recife itself.

■ A two-bedroom, beach-front apartment in the region of Ponta da Pedras costs around US$175,000.

■ A four bedroom house costs around US$245,000.

One of the popular places in Recife is Porto de Galinhas.

■ A three bedroom condominium flat here is around US$90,000.

■ A four bedroom bungalow typically fetches around US$ 200,000.

■ The area also has luxury beach-front villas with pool and separate barbecue area for around US$950,000.

Travelling 9km out of this popular area is Ponta de Serrambi, where prices are cheaper.

■ A six bedroom, beach-front villa can be bought here for US$390,000.

Some of the above types of properties can be found on www.sunshineestates.net. The website does not have a multi-currency conversion facility at the time of writing.

The island of Itamaraca is separated from the mainland by Jaguaribe River and has several beaches that are highly frequented. Other attractions include Forte Orange (Orange Fort) built by the Dutch; Praia do Sossego (Sossego Beach), and Pontal da Ilha.

For those who want to invest a minimum of US$100,000, www.rightmove.co.uk has a number of great value investments available and they advertise prices in sterling only.

■ You could buy a two bedroom apartment for around £14,000 to live in, and buy another two bedroom apartment or a bungalow for the same price, to rent.

■ A three bedroom house in a condominium by the beach costs around £26,000.

■ A four bedroom bungalow close to, but not on, the beach; a small four bedroom house on 120 square metres, or just a plot of land of 360 square metres, with bendy coconut trees, white sand and crystal clear water on the beach, each cost £40,000.

■ A plot of 450 square metres, 200 metres from the beach including a three bedroom bungalow, costs around £32,400.

■ A four bedroom house only 70 metres from the beach, costs around £36,000.

■ 40 metres from the beach, you can buy a five bedroom house for £42,000.

■ A four bedroom, two storey, beach-front house with its own pool has an asking price of £50–60,000.

▨ A 400 square metre building plot on the beach is available for £80,000.

▨ A 600 square metre beach-front plot with a three bedroom bungalow is around £88,000.

▨ A four bedroom villa in a condominium with a pool, pool bar, tennis court and football pitch costs around £110,000.

▨ If you simply want a business opportunity, there are several small hotels (*pousadas*) with no more than 20 bedrooms, available for around £162,000 on the beachfront.

This island is very attractive for the security conscious as you can only go to the north of the island if you are a resident or a guest. There are many such properties available on www.rightmove.co.uk.

The State of Rio Grande do Norte
Natal
The state capital is the city of Natal. This is another state which is becoming very popular with Europeans. Arguably the finest footballer in the world, Kaká, has purchased an apartment in Natal. It has a sunny climate and an average annual temperature of 26°C, 400 kilometres of coastline, with shifting sand dunes, warm, clear water, lakes, coconut groves and, unsurprisingly, is popular with domestic and international tourists all year round.

The Portuguese arrived in the city in 1599 to take over from the French and the Forte dos Reis Magos is still there. There are many good hotels, resorts, restaurants and other leisure facilities. Nearby, Ponte Negra beach provides many simple and small *pousadas*. The Natal coastline is split into two areas by a delta. It used to take 40 minutes to drive around the delta but the Ponte Newton Navarro Bridge completed in November 2007, will no doubt have an impact on property prices and in consequence, large tracts of land are being bought by investors.

▨ Two bedroom, two bathroom, off-plan apartments at Pirangi Beach, have ocean or pool views, pools for children and barbecue areas, plus the apartments have air conditioning. These cost from US$66,000, depending on the view, and are sold by Albany Real Estate LLP. There is some competition, as other developers are offering the same type of accommodation for about the same price, all with an ocean view, see Oyster International developments at www.oyster-international.com.

■ For golfers, Natal Golf Resort has 1–3 bedroom apartments, starting at US$90,000 and going up to US$180,000. These prices reflect the fact that this resort has five 18-hole golf courses, spas, riding facilities, a shopping centre, tennis courts and the Ronaldo Football Academy. These are available from Lifestyle Investments Abroad, see www.lifestyleinvestmentsabroad.com. There are many such resorts in Natal, offering similar facilities. At the top end, there are three bedroom villas in a condominium, available at US$250,000.

■ Away from the condominiums, you can pay US$90,000 for a small, five bedroom bungalow, ten minutes' drive to Ponta Negra Beach.

See www.sunshineestates.net, www.propertyworld.com and www.foxtons.com. Some websites do not have a multi-currency conversion facility.

THE SOUTH

This area comprises the states of Paraná, Santa Catarina and Rio Grande do Sul which are some of the richest states in Brazil. These areas have white sand beaches, tropical forests and snowy mountains and lie in a land of beautifully sharp and contrasting features.

The State of Paraná

This neighbours the state of São Paulo and borders Paraguay and Argentina. Its capital city is Curitiba. It has one of the highest standards of living in Brazil, with a GDP equivalent to Turkey. There is great emphasis on education in the state and there are numerous colleges and universities, which is not altogether surprising, given that the literacy rate is 96%. English and Spanish, as well as Portuguese, is taught in schools.

The state has two geographical regions: a very narrow coastal zone and a high plateau – up to 1,000 metres. The southern and central portions are covered by moist forests and have a uniform, mild, temperate climate. However, although the average annual temperature is an ideal 24°C, it is not unknown for it to climb to 45°C in the summer and to plummet to −5°C in the winter in the city of Foz do Iguaçu.

The largest rivers in the state of Paraná are the Panema and one of its tributaries is the Iguaçu, which has spectacular falls.

Waves of European immigrants settled after 1850, including some from Italy, Germany, Poland and the Ukraine. In the 20th century there was a further influx of immigrants from Japan, China, Arabia, Palestine, Syria and the Lebanon. It has the largest number of east European descendants and is second to São Paulo with the largest number of Japanese and Muslims.

Foz do Iguaçu is the fourth largest city in the state of Paraná. Interestingly, apart from the churches, it has the largest mosque outside of Saudi Arabia and has the largest Buddhist temple in Brazil – Paraná offers a truly tolerant multi-cultural and multi-religious experience.

■ In the countryside, a small, three bedroom, three bathroom house measuring 160 square metres in a plot of 450 square metres can be bought for as little US$30,000.

■ A three bedroom, four bathroom house measuring 280 square metres in a plot of 360 square metres can be bought for around US$100,000.

■ A 1,000 square metre, four bedroom, five bathroom house in a 650 square metre plot with own pool costs US$195,000.

■ A 350 square metre, five bedroom, five bathroom, house in a plot of 650 square metres with a pool costs US$265,000.

■ A luxury 700 square metre, four bedroom, eight bathroom, house in a condominium in its own plot of 845 square metres and a private pool, costs US$600,000.

A good all round website for properties here is www.achaja.com.br.

The State of Santa Catarina

The state capital is the city of Florianópolis and the state neighbours Rio Grande do Sul to the south, Paraná to the north and Argentina to the west. The state has a strong population of German industrialists and Italian farmers. The economy is based on small farms, active industrial parks, large companies and many small businesses.

Some people say that a piece of Germany is carved into Santa Catarina, where the cities of Blumenau, Brusque and Pomerode preserve the culture and tradition of the German immigrants who colonised the region. Travelling south in the state, one will find a distinctive Italian presence, represented by 65% of the state population, producing good wine and homemade food. Urussanga is the capital of Little Italy. German and Italian are spoken in this state.

Florianópolis is an island city boasting one of the lowest crime rates in the world. 60% of the island is a protected nature reserve. However, because of investment in the area, it is seeing a rapid growth rate in development and property values.

- A four bedroom house with five bathrooms on Praia Mole beach can cost up to US$850,000. There are cheaper properties available.

- A three bedroom, beach apartment in a condominium costs around US$185,000.

- A three bedroom house in a condominium with beach views on Praia Mole beach costs US$280,000.

- A four bedroom house an hour from the beach overlooking a lagoon, in a 1,000 square metre plot, costs around US$275,000.

- A 15 bedroom *pousada* in around 1,000 square metres, one hour to the beach, costs around US$425,000.

The State of Rio Grande do Sul

The capital city of this state is Porto Alegre in the middle of *gaucho* or cowboy country. This is a very fertile state, although it is fairly sparsely populated because it is relatively cold, with a plateau region at 800 metres above sea level. It attracts cattle farming, forestry and some of the best honey in the world comes from this mountainous area. There is also fruit and grain production. The climate is generally mild, except on the coastal zone where it is sub-tropical. There are two well-marked seasons, although the transition periods between them (about two months) are described as spring and autumn. During winter (June to September), there is heavy rain and cold westerly winds, lowering the inland temperature to freezing point. Snow is very rare, but ice frequently forms on inland waters over winter nights. The summer is a nominally dry season, but light rains are common and summer temperatures can rise to 35°C.

Typically, a farm in this state, comprising 30 acres, with a main house and two employees' cottages, would cost around US$250,000.

Chapter 6

How to buy real estate

Buying property in Brazil is not straight-
forward, but these guidelines will help you
to survive the experience . . .

RESIDENCY OR INVESTMENT?

Once you are satisfied Brazil is a good investment, you need to decide *why* you
want to buy real estate in Brazil: is it for permanent residency, a holiday home,
rental income or just investment? There are no restrictions (except in relation to
the purchase of large areas of agricultural land) on foreigners buying land and
property in Brazil in their own names. However, if you do buy without applying
for permanent residency, be aware that you will be, strictly speaking, limited to
spending a maximum of six months of a year in Brazil.

PROCESSES

Once you have decided on the purpose of buying in Brazil, you will then need to
find the correct means for doing so. Land in Brazil is subject to state registration.
The location of the local land registry can be found from the offices of the *prefeitura*
(local authority). It is necessary, having found a property to purchase, to have
searches done in the court system and company registry to find out whether the
title is encumbered by unpaid taxes, law suits against the owner (whether an
individual or a company) or any dispute as to title. It is important to exercise the
utmost care and never could the Latin maxim *caveat emptor* (let the buyer beware)
have a better application.

Estate agents in Brazil have to be members of a professional organisation and carry a membership and identification card with a number called a CRECI number, establishing their qualifications and right to practise. Every agent should be able to produce his or her card on request for inspection. Often these agents are perfectly well qualified to carry out all necessary searches, prepare the documents and deal with the money transfers.

BUYING THROUGH YOUR OWN COMPANY

If you are buying property through a Brazilian company established by yourself for the purpose of securing permanent residency, it is of the utmost importance that you follow procedures prescribed by the Banco Central do Brasil. These lay down procedures for the transfer, tracing and certification of funds, which must come from abroad and demonstrably be an inward investment by yourself into the company.

Except for dependents, the minimum amount of investment in the company per person is the equivalent of US$50,000. On sums brought into Brazil by bank transfers, there is a tax of 0.38%. It used to be the case that you had to invest US$250,000 and also to employ at least ten Brazilian workers to qualify for permanent residency status. However, this has been lowered to the level stated and there is no longer a need to employ anyone. Some professionals here have not caught up with this change and you need to ensure that the advisers that you use are on the ball.

Brazilian lawyers are called *advogados* (broadly translating to advocates) and are theoretically qualified to handle both court work and paper work. If you decide to use a Brazilian lawyer (and you will really need to do so to establish a Brazilian company), be prepared for the fact that many of them set *gringo* levels of fees for foreigners, which few but the richest Brazilians could possibly afford: you will end up paying fees equivalent to, or more than, those payable in Western Europe and North America to effect even simple land transactions.

PROPERTY TAXES

When you register the title to the land, there is a purchase tax called ITBI, which is 2% of the value of the purchase. In addition, in relation to some ocean-front properties, there is another tax called marine tax (*laudemeo*) which is 5% of the *land* value (disregarding the value of the buildings), according to a statutory valuation. There is, additionally, an annual local tax levied by the *prefeitura* for the provision of local services, such as rubbish collection, roads, schools, medical centres, hospitals and so forth. The local tax depends on the size of the house and varies, but it is not a great deal. If you sell the house, there is a capital gains tax of 15% for residents, which is not applicable if the proceeds are reinvested. Personal income tax in Brazil (which applies on world-wide income if you are resident in Brazil) is graduated up to a maximum of 25%.

IMPORT DUTIES

There are import duties which range between 0% and 22.5% on certain goods (higher rates apply to such things as automobiles). There is no duty on importing household goods from storage, provided you have a right to bring them into the country as a permanent resident. You must bring the goods into the country not less than three months and not more than six months, after obtaining your visa. Any good relocation firm will be able to advise on what may or may not be brought into the country. Shipping by air is not a good idea as shipping anything in this way, except medical supplies for your own consumption, attracts a tariff of 60% on the free on board value between US$51 and US$3,000. Personal importation of cigarettes and alcohol is banned. Personal goods, comprising passenger baggage, are exempt from tax. However, if you transfer residency to Brazil you will be exempt from paying import duties as long as you gain permission from the Brazilian Consulate in the country of origin.

BE CAUTIOUS!

When you are buying real estate in Brazil there are two main problems to note. Firstly, there are estate agents advertising properties on the internet and they often seek to charge the buyer a commission of up to 5%, whereas when buying through a Brazilian agent in Brazil it is only the vendor who pays commission. Secondly, never use an *advogado* unless they have been personally recommended to you by someone you know and trust, or who is on a list held by a Consulate General, or is a member of an internationally-recognised firm of lawyers. It is also worth noting that we know of at least one instance where property has been advertised for sale fraudulently and unsuspecting foreigners have transferred funds to Brazil whereupon the 'vendor' has run off with the money, leaving no trace – there being no title to the property for sale. One of the *advogados* whom we used tried to dupe us into transferring him an extra R$10,000 to pay taxes which he had vastly inflated in order to defraud us. In the event, he simply failed to account to us for R$8,000 which he already had. We counted our lucky stars that, for some reason, he had not chosen to run off with much more. When such things happen, there is little point in expecting much redress from the police or the professional organisations. They will take statements and contact details and then, one suspects, file it all in the cylindrical filing cabinet under the desk or, at best in the tray marked 'LBW' – Let the Blighters Wait.

Even when you are dealing with Brazilian professionals, do not be surprised if they do not turn up for a pre-arranged meeting, although you have travelled a couple of hours to keep an appointment. Do not be surprised either if they do not trouble to call you to cancel. After a stiff protest on an answer phone or by e-mail, they will reply after a couple of days with a long shaggy-dog story about a dead relative and a mad rush across the country to console an aged widow or something of the kind. The apologies will be profuse and insincere – because some (not all, but some) do this kind of thing as a matter of course. If you express disbelief and further disappointment, they may well shrug and smile resignedly and say 'This is Brazil'.

Chapter 7

Living in Brazil

Understanding everyday living in Brazil will make your life here more enjoyable. The main tip: go with the flow.

THE REAL COST OF LIVING IN BRAZIL

The currency of Brazil is the Brazilian Real (plural Reis) – R$ (pronounced respectively, 'Hayawl' and 'He'eyezh') and rough conversion rates, at the time of writing, are R$1 = $US0.5, GB£0.25, €0.375 or US$1 = R$1.95, GB£1 = R$3.94 and €1 = R$2.66. The Real is currently strong against these and other currencies. In 2005, the exchange rate to the GB£ was R$5 = GB£1.

Doing a comparison of two families living in a five bedroom beach house which has been purchased for cash, produces the following:

A frugal family can survive on just over R$1,000 a month and an extravagant family would be spending in excess of R$6,000.

Utilities
Water
Water comes in various ways, for various purposes: it comes bottled (most expensive) for drinking and is about R$4 for a 20 litre tub which you invert over a simple dispenser or a more expensive one with a cooler. There is street water which some *prefeituras* provide through certain street pipes several days a week and which is siphoned off on a meter system and stored in underground cisterns. This is quite cheap – about R$15 for 10,000 litres and is drinkable. There is artesian well water which is good enough for bathing and washing, but you would

not want to drink it – not least because each house has its own sewerage system – basically a deep pit which filters and drains the effluent away into the earth. Well water costs the amount of the electricity to raise it by pump into storage cisterns.

Gas

Gas comes in cylinders which cost about R$35 each for the standard size and, if just used for cooking, last a reasonable length of time.

Electricity

Electricity is supplied by a company called Ampla and is expensive. For a house as described above, without the mitigation of cost occasioned by solar panels, the charge per month is likely to be in the region of R$350 (assuming use of a refrigerator, iron, televisions, computers and normal lighting).

Telephone

Landline telephone services are connected through Embratel, Telemar and Inmartel. For normal usage making national and international calls to landlines and mobiles the approximate cost is in the region of R$400 a month. A frugal family would use a local pay-as-you-go mobile and the computer. There are also prepaid cards which provide heavily discounted calls and may be purchased (as may mobile phone cards) at news stands, in some shops and the post office (*correios*). Public payphones are situated all over the place and take prepaid cards which you slide into a reader.

Internet

There are various internet suppliers (such as Netterra, which provides an excellent service) and the cost depends on the speed of connection which can be up to 150mbps and beyond – between R$75 and R$100+. There are also many internet cafés which provide cheap access to the internet for occasional users.

Domestic staff

Domestic staff cost about R$500 a month per person and each worker will work around eight to nine hours a day for five or six days a week and will do the cooking, cleaning, scrubbing, brushing, washing, ironing, etc. Details of workers' rights are given later in the chapter.

Alcohol and cigarettes

Alcohol and cigarettes are cheap in the retail shops, although price of alcohol in smart restaurants and hotels rivals those of North America and West Europe. In the shops there is reasonable red and white wine from Southern Brazil (outside the tropics) where grapes seem to grow tolerably well. One very common wine is Almaden and it costs around R$15 a bottle. There is also available better Chilean and Argentinean wine which can cost up to R$40 a bottle. Imported wine from Italy, France and Portugal is available. Proper Spanish sherry is very difficult to come by, but red and white ports are sold. Locally-made spirits such as gin (made under the English brand name Seager's) is about R$15 a litre. Imported spirits are much more expensive. Cigarettes are typically R$2.50 a packet. Imported cigars are at international prices. Beer – lager by Skol, Brahmin Chopp and Antarctica – is cheap. Malt beer and black beer are about R$1.5 for a small bottle.

A boozy, moderately extravagant family will spend R$1,000 a month on alcohol; whereas beer-drinking moderates will spend R$400 a month.

Tea and coffee

Tea (except green tea) is not worth drinking unless it is imported. Although there is a local brand which boasts the name 'Lipton', Sir Thomas would turn in his grave to behold it. Even though the song tells us that 'There's an awful lot of coffee in Brazil', it seems that the best is exported (unlike in Colombia where the best is kept for the Colombians).

Running a car

There are three different fuels in Brazil: petrol (*gasolina*), alcohol (*alcool*) and gas. Petrol is the most expensive, followed by *alcool* and then gas. There is an annual emissions check carried out on all cars (well, supposed to be carried out on all cars).

A litre of *gasolina* from Petrobras (Brazilian company) costs R$ 2.79 and *alcool* (which has been banned in USA because it is so cheap) costs R$1.75 a litre.

Insurance can be arranged through the bank, although it doesn't appear to be compulsory.

Medical care

There are free (and efficient) local walk-in health centres (with doctors and nurses) and free basic hospitals which can set a broken bone in old-fashioned plaster. However, there is no nationally-organised health service and it is best to secure family health insurance which can be had for around R$300 a month to cover the cost of private medical care and private hospital treatment.

Emergency services

Most areas also have a fire service (*bombeiros*) and a free ambulance service (*ambulancia*).

The police force in Brazil is divided into four main sections:

■ Policia Civil is the State Civil Police Department – each of the states of Brazil have their own State Civil Police Department that conducts investigations, forensics and detective work involving criminal activity in the state.

■ Policia Militar – The Military Police is considered a preventative, state-controlled police force, mainly used for riot control, internal affairs detachments and special operations deployment. It is also an auxiliary and reserve of the federal military forces. Some states have a cavalry unit.

■ Policia Rodoviaria Federal – The Federal Highway Police patrol the federal highways and carry two gun holsters, one strapped on each thigh.

■ Policia Federal – The Federal Police investigate crimes against the government and its organs, combat terrorism, international drug trafficking and immigration and border control.

Telephone numbers for the emergency services are:

■ Fire brigade: 193;

■ Ambulance: 192;

■ Police: 190.

Home entertainment

Television sets, radios, hi-fi and electronic equipment (except computers which are the same price as in North America and Western Europe) cost the same in Reis as they do in US$ and GB£ (for example, if a medium size and quality television costs £400 in the UK, it will cost R$400 in Brazil.) Sky costs about R$100 a month: if you enjoy watching television, you will need this as Brazilian TV is dire – news programmes, punctuated with soaps (*novellas*), blind date-type programmes and one channel devoted to cattle! DVDs cost R$12–30 each, depending on the film, or they can be rented on a daily basis for R$3–4. There are cinemas in some bigger centres with many films in English/American. The cost of entry is about R$8 per person.

House upkeep

If you buy a house right on the Atlantic coast, be prepared for a lot of maintenance because of the strong winds (the famous trade winds), sea air and the spume which the Brazilians call *marazia* which is extremely corrosive, especially of metal; although the oily Brazilian hardwoods fare rather better. Before you plant a garden facing the sea you will need advice on which plants will withstand the sea air: many do not – our roses, fruit trees, orchids, bougainvillea and other tender items were burnt to a crisp. House insurance against all the usual risks is based, ultimately, on the cost of rebuilding and the premium is set at about one thousandth of this cost. Insuring against theft of goods is difficult and levels of insurance offered are low. The banks all offer house insurance.

Groceries and home cooking

Almost every house has a barbecue (*churrascaria*) which is in regular use for beef, pork sausage, salami, chicken and fish. Seafood is readily available and includes crab, lobster, prawns, wet fish like snapper, bass, sole and other big, oily fish with local names, such as *pargo* and *anchova*. Meat and fish are cheap. Large prawns are R$12–13 per kilo.

Beef is a favourite meat and is very good; lamb is not easily obtainable everywhere; there is bacon and ham (pig and turkey) and, of course, chicken. The staple Brazilian diet comprises: rice, beans, eggs and *farofa* (grated manioc). *Farofa* is sometimes made into *feijoada* by mixing in chopped pig offal and end pieces (we have heard that this includes *all* pieces!).

Fruit is very, very cheap and often you can pick it off the wild trees overhanging public roads – coconuts, mango, papaya, Japanese medlars, bananas (of which there are many different types, including savoury varieties, which are frittered and eaten with meat). There are passion fruit, strawberries, guava, avocadoes, tomatoes, potatoes, manioc, cabbage, salad vegetables, acerola, oranges, limes, jack fruit, tangerines, satsumas, cashew fruit and nuts, pineapple, melon, apples, pears and grapes.

Great British favourites

There are no baked beans, Marmite or Bovril, other than at exorbitant prices in big cities. The Brazilians favour a yellow mousetrap cheese which they eat sliced in a pale imitation of French bread. However, there are good imitations of cheddar, Gorgonzola, Roquefort, smoked cheese, Edam and others with a European derivation. The biscuits are very good as is the chocolate; although the Brazilians have yet to learn the art of making great gum or boiled sweets and candy; caramel and toffee are so-so. Ice cream is of general North American and Western European standard and, although not at the luxury end of the market in terms of quality, ice creams are expensive: a standard supermarket tub is about R$15.

Clothing

Ordinary Brazilians don't wear much in the way of clothes: sandals, flip-flops on the feet, shorts and a tee shirt or singlet are usual, everyday wear for everybody, except professionals, bankers, businessmen and civil servants. No foreigner would much desire many of the clothes on offer. However, they are very cheap; between about a half to a quarter of the cost of similar items in North America and Europe. Suits, shirts, ties and city shoes are generally nothing like the same standard as those from London, Paris or New York. Therefore, do your serious clothes shopping in your normal places.

Schools

These are paid for out of local taxes and for children of pre-school age the schooling is free. For children aged 6–14 education is free and compulsory. Higher education, including at degree level is free at state universities. There are private English and American schools, see Chapter 8 for details.

EMPLOYING DOMESTIC STAFF IN BRAZIL

This section is intended to provide guidance only and does not constitute legal advice. Appropriate legal advice should be sought. It should be read in the light of the general remarks about conduct and ethics in Brazil: whoever you engage and under whatever contract, expect there to be a good chance of petty theft of little bits and pieces: cleaning materials, crockery and cutlery and any apparent 'surfeit' of your own personal clothing.

There are two ways of engaging staff. The first is by way of a standard contract of employment, which may be in writing or oral. The second is by way of engaging someone who is self employed and free to provide the services, to the required standard, through themselves or someone else. The test whether someone is an employee (under a contract for service) or self employed (under a service rendering agreement) is simply a question of the degree of control over the service provider. However, for the purposes of this book, it is assumed that the employer will be employing domestic staff who are, usually, employees.

Getting references seems like a good idea but remember that Brazil is a socialist republic and workers' rights are paramount. Any former employer who even suggests dishonesty in a former employee is likely to find himself facing a claim for damages – and woe betide that ex-employer who cannot fully and plainly demonstrate his claim. Accordingly, view all references with suspicion and read between the lines – better still, telephone the ex-employer for an off-the-record chat.

Brazilian domestic labourers enjoy good employee protection. They have social rights, guaranteed by the Constitution and the CLT – the Consolidation of Brazilian Labour Laws. These rights may not be over-ridden by private agreement.

Importantly, there is the basic minimum wage which at the moment is R$380 per month. Most people pay 1.5 times the basic minimum wage. There is also a requirement for the employer to pay 8.5% of the wage into a fund for the employee's benefit (for severance pay and social security benefits). Every employee is also entitled to a 13th month of every annual wage or a proportionate part (according to time worked), payable as a Christmas bonus. They are entitled to 30 days' paid holiday a year and a cash bonus of 33% of salary for that month on top.

It is normal to engage someone by signing their Labour Card and also agreeing to the terms in the books of the employer or employing company.

Employees may be dismissed summarily for just cause – such as stealing – but beware: you need strict proof of the felony. If you do not have it, be prepared to pay out for dismissal without cause. This means that you will need to give 30 days' notice (or pay in lieu), pay all outstanding salary, pay a proportion of the 13th month's extra salary and a proportion of the 33% vacation pay for the month's holiday. You will have to pay double the accrued (untaken) vacation and give release of the FGTS severance pay plus an additional 40% of the accrued employer's deposits and another 10% for good measure.

If an employee resigns, they are entitled to the same as above, except for pay in lieu of notice, the release of the severance pay funds and additional sums described. If the employee has less than a year's service, there are also no vacation rights.

There are also rights to maternity and paternity pay, prescribed rights to overtime pay, a special night-shift rate, a right to a food and travel allowance and a right to one day off a week (preferably a Sunday).

So, if you do employ a Brazilian employee, it is best to stick to the bargain: you have been warned!

GOING OUT AND ENTERTAINMENT

Cuisine

As Brazil's population comprises an interesting mix of people of Portuguese, African, Italian, German, Syrian, Lebanese and Asian origin, this produces a rich heritage in terms of cuisine, producing a diversity of cooking styles.

The North

Culturally, the Amazon basin is populated by Amerindians and people of mixed Indian and Portuguese ancestry living on a diet of fish, root vegetables, such as manioc, yams, peanuts and tropical fruits such as bananas. *Caruru do Para* is a dish comprising dried shrimps, okra, onion, tomatoes and coriander all made in a pot.

The North East

Inland, the North East region is semi-arid and used for cattle rearing. The foods here typically include foods such as dried meat – especially goat, rice, beans, manioc and corn meal. On the fertile coastal plains, the influence is more Afro-Bahian which has evolved from plantation cooks, improvising on African, Indian and traditional Portuguese dishes, drawing on locally-available ingredients. On other coastal plains, the influence on foods is less African and the staple diet comprises seafood, shell fish and tropical fruits.

The Central West

The region comprises open dry savannahs, with woodlands in the north. Pantanal is regarded as one of the finest game and fishing regions on Earth. There are many rivers in the region and vast ranches. Consequently, fish from these rivers and beef dominate the menu. In addition, agricultural crops such as soy beans, rice, corn and manioc are commonly consumed.

THE SOUTH EAST

This is the industrial part of Brazil and home to several distinctive styles of cooking. Around Minas Gerais, the main dishes include corn, pork, beans and local soft cheeses. Around Rio de Janeiro and São Paulo a dish of Bahian origin, called *feijoada* is very popular. Another popular dish in this region is *arroz feijao* which is rice and beans (sometimes with a fried egg on the top). Traditionally, Rio de Janeiro is home to the black bean, São Paulo is home to the red or white bean and Minas Gerais to the red and the black bean. In São Paulo, the influence of European and North African immigrants is strong. The majority of them consume Italian, Portuguese, Spanish and Arabian food.

The South

This is home to the national cuisine of the *gaucho* (cowboy), comprising dishes made from salt or sun-dried meats and *churrasco* (barbecue). The immigrant farming population of the south developed a wheat-based diet and introduced wine, leafy vegetables and dairy products to the Brazilian diet.

Typical Brazilian foods

Beans (*feijao*) appear on the table daily. Some people say that the black bean is the national bean of Brazil. Coconuts are important throughout the country, used in soups, cocktails, poultry, fish and shellfish cooking as well as in sweet dishes. The coconut used is from the unripe green coconut, the ripe yellow or brown coconut and may be grated. Dried, salted cod, known as *bacalhau*, introduced by the Portuguese, is used in soups, main courses and savoury puddings. For those from the northern hemisphere who are used to fresh cod, this dried, salted variety is certainly different. Dried shrimps (*camarao seco*) are used in many dishes from the northern regions of the country. Rice (*arroz Brasileiro*) dishes are made with sautéed garlic and oil. Toasted manioc meal (*farofa*) is manioc flour, lightly sautéed in butter.

The *acai* (pronounced 'ah-sigh-ee') berry was the staple diet for the Amazonian tribes and recently has been sold in parts of North America and Europe as the new, number one superfood. Unfortunately the fruit has to be processed within 24 hours otherwise it loses its nutritional value. Therefore, it is usually sold in a slushy form and one might think that people in Rio de Janeiro clutching a beaker full of a purple-looking sorbet are gorging themselves on ice cream. This is not so. The superfood, which resembles the shape and size of a grape, is purple in colour and tastes like chocolate-coated cherries. In Rio, it is usually mixed with other fruit such as banana, served with a layer of grated nuts or granola and smeared with a layer of syrup.

Traditionally, Brazilians used the *acai* berry to treat digestive disorders and skin conditions, but recently there has been much interest suggesting that the *acai* berry can have a positive effect on treating other disorders including diabetes, neurological diseases, raised cholesterol levels and even cancer. Nutritionally, the berry is said to have high levels of calcium, antioxidants, omega-3 fatty acids, glucosamine and macro-minerals.

SAFETY AND SECURITY

There is no doubt that Brazil has a reputation as a dangerous country, where violent crime is rife. There is no smoke without fire, and it certainly can be a dangerous place where crimes of robbery and opportunistic theft occur with depressing frequency.

In the cities

The major cities of Brazil have *favelas* which are shanty towns built anyhow by the landless people, often the descendants of former slaves, who were given land by the government in order to provide housing as best they could for themselves. These *favelas* are plainly visible even in central parts of Rio de Janeiro and in and around other major cities. However, they are communities, with electric lighting, roads, shops and even banks. They are sometimes centres of drug-dealing and shoot-outs between rival gangs and between gangs and the police. For foreigners, these places are definitely 'no go' areas; if you venture into them, there is a very fair chance that you will be robbed, seriously assaulted or caught in cross-fire. In any event, when going into any large centres of population, it is as well to appear as inconspicuous as possible and it is certainly wise not to display jewellery and designer labels, or to carry bags which are just ripe for snatching. Bum bags or money belts are a good idea – better still, have zipped pouches securely strapped to your lower legs. There is no need to carry your original passport – a photocopy is acceptable for identification purposes.

Never take out money on the street. If you can afford it, use a driver with a car to drop you at the places you need to go, wait for you or pick you up. In major centres there are tourist police who have their own department and speak English. Having said this, if you keep to safer areas (where there are usually plenty of police in evidence, sometimes in kiosks on the pavements) and walk directly and purposefully to and from your destinations, looking as though you know what you are about, and keeping a weather eye open for dodgy-looking loiterers, you will be best equipped to get by safely.

Outside of the cities

Out of the major centres, smaller towns are generally safe, even safer than similar centres of population in the UK. In provincial centres in Brazil, the greatest risk is leaving your gate and doors unlocked, giving an opportunity for someone to nip in and out with a television set, carelessly placed money or other valuables. Certainly, if you leave anything of value lying around in a public place, in a matter of minutes it will be gone. An interesting consequence of this is that if you want to get rid of old furniture or anything of the kind, just leave it on the pavement. It will disappear without the effort and expense of hiring someone to take it to the dump for you.

Home and personal security

House and car alarms are a good idea, as well as outside security lights. Most people have a guard dog – some have more than one. Personal alarms are available but, frankly, if you are the victim of a snatch and run, they'll be off before you know what has happened. Window bars on ground-floor house windows are usual and nearly every substantial house is surrounded by a high wall and gates. Retractable metal grills are also advisable. Make sure that you have the telephone numbers of the emergency services to hand. Battery chargeable walk-and-talk telephones are sold and you can keep one of these by the bed.

Wildlife

So far as dangerous creatures are concerned, there are in rural areas, venomous snakes (mainly coral snakes); there are also various constrictors. Off the coast of northern Brazil, sharks are a problem in the sea, but not generally as far south as Rio de Janeiro. There are also large black wasps and millipedes (which can inflict a nasty sting and bite) but, outside of the jungle, you are fairly safe from animal harm.

Vaccinations

So far as vaccinations are concerned, commonly recommended vaccinations for Brazil are:

- hepatitis A;

- yellow fever (recommended for the states of Acre, Amapá, Amazonas, Goiás, Maranhão, Mato Grosso, Mato Grosso do Sul, Minais Gerais, Pará, Rondônia, Roraima and Tocantins; also compulsory if you arrive from a fever infected area such as Africa or the Americas);

- hepatitis B (especially if visiting for more than six months);

- rabies (if you may have direct contact with animals);

- plus tetanus, diphtheria, rubella, polio and chicken pox.

Malaria is a risk most common in the northern parts of Brazil and tablets are recommended. There is also Dengue (breakbone) fever, but there is no vaccination – only avoidance of the mosquito which spreads it – and no real treatment except rest.

Maybe it goes without saying to drink only bottled water.

PUBLIC AND PRIVATE TRANSPORT WITHIN BRAZIL

As may be expected, in a country which provides major tourist attractions, there are many means of transport around Brazil. The biggest issue is safety.

Air travel

Brazil's airlines are Varig (www.varig.com.br) and TAM (www.tam.com.br). These are the only airlines which offer air passes, allowing visitors to fly around the country easily. Bear in mind that air travel in Brazil can be expensive, as there is a departure tax (currently about US$40). If you wish to see a reasonable extent of Brazil, you will need to take a domestic flight or two. There are about 100 national airports connecting the major cities of each state; in addition to these, there are small landing grounds for light aircraft scattered all over the place.

Buses (onibus)

These are the cheapest means of transport in Brazil. For example, a journey from Saquarema to Rio de Janeiro by bus travels over the mountain roads and the Rio-Niteroi Bridge and so, although it is only 50 miles, it takes about two hours. However, it only costs between R$8 and R$10. A better route would be to travel to Niteroi by bus and then take the hydrofoil (between R$3 and 4) across the bay (a few minutes) and then on into central Rio by cab or bus. Buses are also the most reliable form of transport and can take passengers from all the major cities and towns to many out-lying districts, including the heart of the Amazon jungle.

It is not uncommon in some of the more remote areas when travelling at night, for there to be an accident, as Brazil's roads leave a great deal to be desired. Moreover, the vehicles themselves are often not particularly safe and the standard of driving also is below par, giving rise to the expression 'Barber!', meaning, presumably, someone who cuts you up. Beside the fact that Brazilians drive on the right hand side (most of the time), note that, if a driver flashes his lights at you, he means, 'I am coming on regardless'. In cities, especially around the more dangerous quarters (*favelas*) at night, it is customary for red traffic lights to be ignored.

You will find that the state of the roads is, in many places, very bad; pavements are often non-existent or uneven and broken. Cyclists (sometimes also people on motorbikes and in cars) travel on major roads with no lights, and pedestrians do not have reflectors on their clothing. Seat belts and crash helmets are compulsory but many do not abide by the law, and it is not at all unusual to see up to four people perched on a bicycle or motorbike.

There are striped road crossings, but pedestrians should wait for a red light to stop the traffic before crossing as pedestrians do not have priority. There is no law against jay walking.

Trains

Brazilian trains are not well-maintained and the infrastructure lacks investment. Nevertheless, if dramatic scenery is what you are after, a train journey is to be recommended.

Car hire

It is not recommended to hire cars unless you really know what you are doing as road safety is poor. However, you can readily hire a driver and car for a 12- or 13-hour day for approximately R$300 – which is equivalent to US$150 or GB£75. Sometimes, you will find that these drivers will go out of their way to help you. The cost in local terms is quite high, bearing in mind the minimum wage in Brazil. However, as with any other service in Brazil, it is as well to proceed by way of personal introduction, by a known, trustworthy third party who will stake their reputation on the recommendation of the driver in question. The age and state of the car, as well as the driving skills, will speak volumes. Therefore try a few out before you embark on a long journey. Sometimes, in remote areas, which are quite safe in the daytime, armed bandits stalk the roads at night, and you had better keep away. Good drivers will know their areas and avoid danger zones.

Car ownership

If you decide to spend any length of time in Brazil you will need to think about owning a car. A typical second-hand VW Gol (the Brazilian version of the VW Golf) with four doors costs about R$10,000 or US$5,000 or GB£2,500. An EU licence, strictly speaking, has to be translated in case you are stopped by the police, but is valid for driving in Brazil. Imported cars tend to be more expensive than those manufactured in Brazil and there is also the obvious problem in readily getting spare parts.

Boat and river travel

This is strictly for the more adventurous, especially for those with good travel health insurance. However, this represents one of the most spectacular ways in which to travel. The boat ferries and the hydrofoil between Rio de Janeiro and Niteroi (a city on the north side of the bay) are quite safe and provide much speedier access out of Rio (towards the Region of the Lagoons), than the Rio-Niteroi Bridge, which often suffers from severe congestion.

Trams

There are trams in some major cities – but these are generally used by the fairly poor and the risk of robbery is high.

INTERNATIONAL PORTS AND AIRPORTS

Major sea ports in Brazil include:

- Rio de Janeiro;

- Rio Grande;

- San Sebastiao;

- Santos;

- Sepetiba Terminal;

- Tubarao;

- Vitória;

- Gebig;

- Itaqai.

Major international airports include:

- Galeao Antonio Carlos Jobim in Rio de Janeiro;

- Guarulhos International Airport and Congonhas International Airport in São Paulo;

- Presidente Juscelino Kubitschek International Airport in Brasília;

- Hercilio Luz International Airport, Santa Catarina, Florianópolis;

- International Deputado Luis Eduardo Magalhaes in Salvador;

- Salgado Filho International Airport in Porto Alegre. Rio Grande do Sul;

- Pinto Martins International Airport, Fortaleza, Ceará;

- Presidente Castro Pinto International Airport, João Pessoa, Paraíba;

- Augusto Severo International Airport, Natal, Rio Grande do Norte;

- Guararapes/ Gilberto Freyre International Airport, Recife, Pernambuco.

If you are travelling from Europe travel time increases if you stop off in Lisbon with TAP airline or in Madrid with Iberia airline. Brazil is so vast that you will be over northern Brazil for a couple of hours before you reach Rio. Some airlines travel to Rio via São Paulo, which is also best avoided, unless you desperately want a cheaper ticket.

There are many local and national airports because road and rail alternatives are not first rate. There are 29,295km of railways and 1,751,000km of roads of which only 96,000km is metalled.

COMMUNICATIONS AND MEDIA

Voice communication

As already described, Brazil is an enormous country with the associated need for good internal and external communications. Readily available means of communication include:

■ landline telephones (38 million in use);

■ satellite telephones;

■ mobile phones (here called a cellular telephone – 86 million in use);

■ fax machines;

■ internet (both cable and satellite), which enables cheap computer-to-telephone calls to be made anywhere in the world and free computer-to-computer calls (including video conferencing), by means of free downloadable systems provided by such providers as Yahoo Messenger, Skype and MSN Messenger.

Costs are equivalent to those in Western Europe.

Post

There is a reasonable postal system, which includes national registered post (called *sedex*) and international registered post (*registrado urgente*). The FedEx courier service also operates within a reasonable distance of major centres.

Television

There are 138 television broadcasting stations receivable in Brazil and 1,661 radio stations.

BANKING IN BRAZIL

ATMs of Banco Bradesco allow the use of a range of international credit, debit and cash cards, such as VISA, MasterCard and Cirrus. There are small charges imposed for the use of these cards and converting the money, but no tax imposed on withdrawals. It is far more convenient to use ATMs than travellers' cheques or converting foreign currency which you can cash only in large centres, and often at very unfavourable rates. Permitted withdrawal amounts are either R$600 or R$1,000 per card per day, depending on the machine: the kiosks or machines in shops at petrol stations allow R$1,000 whilst those in the banks have a R$600 limit. In the banks, use the machines with the dark blue spot above them. Sometimes, you need to persevere. The service is available in English and the machine recognises your card and gives you an English option. Even the machines that normally allow only R$600 per card per day will often allow a second withdrawal, even if the total thus exceeds the daily allowance.

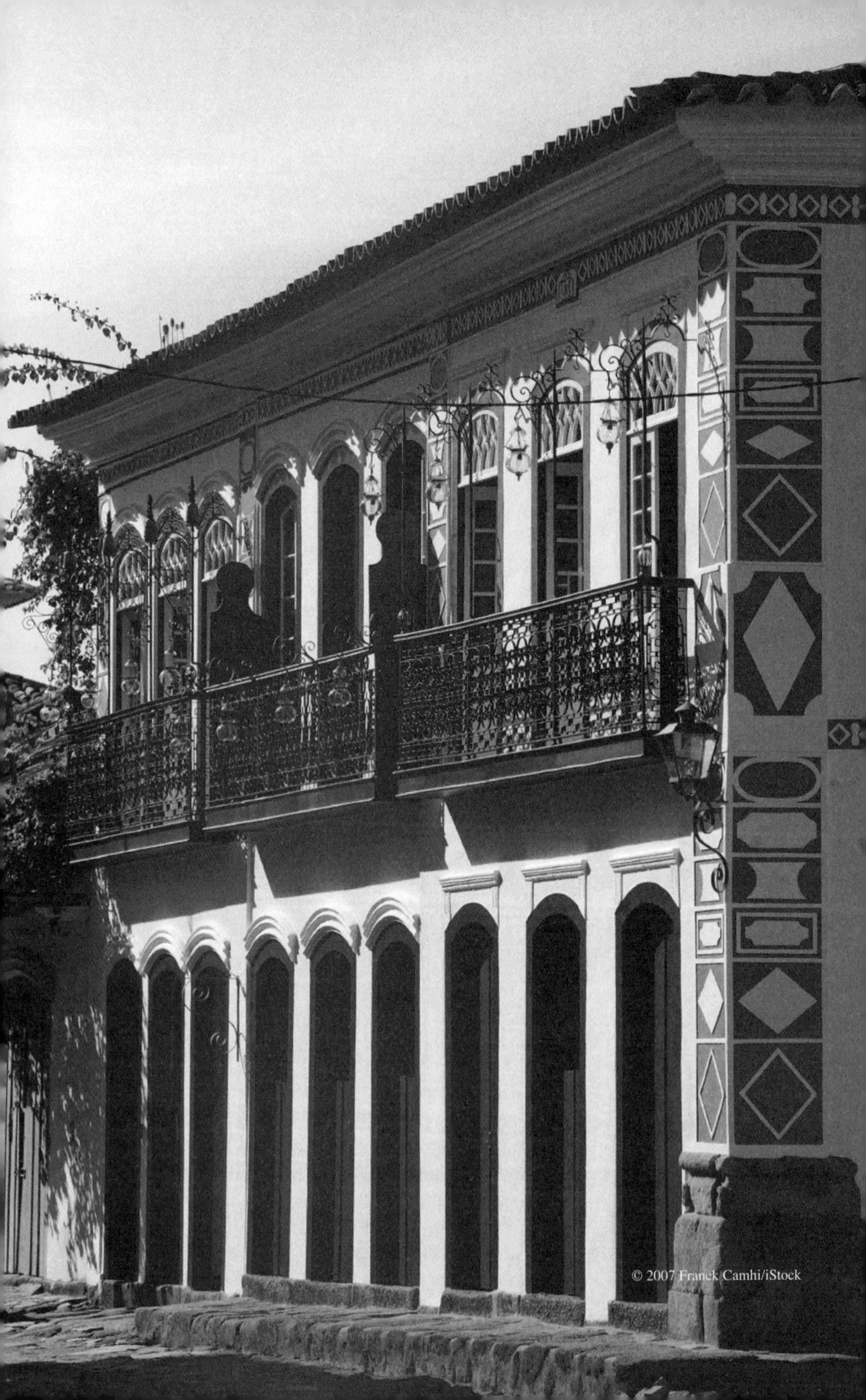

Chapter 8

Private education

The reality is that most — if not all — expats will want to use the private rather than the state system of education whilst living in Brazil.

It is generally acknowledged that lack of education and poverty go hand in hand, as is the case in Brazil. Although the government claims to provide free and compulsory public education, the exception proves the rule and most educated Brazilians have been educated privately and send their children to private schools. For this reason, only the private schools have been mentioned below.

Higher education in Brazil remains the preserve of the middle and upper classes. Nearly all the students at university arrive via private schools.

SCHOOLS IN RIO DE JANEIRO

The British School of Rio de Janeiro – www.britishschool.g12.br
The school was founded in 1924 by Sir Alexander Mackenzie. By 1999 it had earned the Award of Accreditation from the European Council of International Schools (ECIS).

There is a nursery unit in Botafogo. The primary school and the first year of secondary school are also based in Botafogo. Secondary classes are based in the neighbourhood of Urca, a few minutes from Sugar Loaf Mountain. A shuttle service runs between the two sites several times a day. The Urca neighbourhood has two universities and a library.

The curriculum for the primary education sector is based on the national curriculum for England. The secondary school prepares the students for the Cambridge International General Certificate of Secondary Education and offers a full International Baccalaureate for classes ten and 11.

The tuition fees payable per month vary between R$1,756 to R$ 2,955 from pre-nursery to class 11.

Escola Americana do Rio de Janeiro – www.earj.com.br

See AASSA section below for full details.

SCHOOLS IN SÃO PAULO

The St Nicholas International School – www.stnicholas.com.br

The St Nicholas School began in 1980 with a small nursery and now has 400 pupils from 18 months to 18 years and 100 staff.

Students are prepared for the International Baccalaureate as well as the English national curriculum for KS1 to KS3.

The school is based in the heart of São Paulo and there are many school buses. Tuition fees are available on request.

St Paul's School – www.stpauls.br

The school was formally opened in 1926, although it can be traced as far back as 1867 to the arrival of British railway employees. It is now regarded as an Anglo-Brazilian bilingual and bicultural school.

Situated in a 1.8-hectare site in the leafy neighbourhood of Jardins, it has an excellent academic reputation which rivals the best of schools in Brazil and the UK.

The pre-preparatory school is organised into 12 classes. The preparatory school numbers around 350 aged six to 11 years. At senior school students are prepared for the International General Certificate of Secondary Education (IGCSE) and the International Baccalaureate in the sixth form.

Tuition fees are available on request.

Chapel International School-www.chapelschool.com

See AASSA section below for full details.

AASSA SCHOOLS IN BRAZIL

The Association of American Schools in South America (AASSA) is a not-for-profit organisation serving over 40 schools in South America and offshore islands.

There are 11 such schools in Brazil and, although there is great variance in size, they are all college preparatory institutions offering a predominantly American curriculum taught in English. All AASSA schools are fully accredited by the Southern Association of Colleges and Schools and an increasing number of the schools offer the International Baccalaureate programme.

Escola Americana do Rio de Janeiro – www.earj.com.br

The Escola Americana do Rio de Janeiro offers an English-language matriculation culminating in an American diploma. As an option, students may enrol instead for the International Baccalaureate. Additionally, students born in Brazil engage in a course in Portuguese, including the Brazilian culture and history, culminating in a Portuguese diploma.

The school has two sites, one for pre-nursery to kindergarten based in Jardim Oceanica, and another from nursery through to upper school in the Gavea neighbourhood. The school operates a bus service to and from Ipanema, Leblon, Lagoa, Jardim Botanico, São Conrado, Barra da Tijuca, Itanhanga, Recreio, Copacabana, Leme, Flamengo, Catete, Urca, Laranjeiras, and Botafogo.

The monthly tuition fees vary between R$2,054 to R$4,611 from pre-nursery to upper school.

Our Lady of Mercy School, Rio de Janeiro – www.olmrio.org

Our Lady of Mercy School, Rio de Janeiro, is an accredited English language, American and Brazilian curriculum school at the cutting edge of an education programme based on Catholic principles. It can trace its roots back to 1919 with 'Our Lady of Mercy Society'. It lies between the Sugar Loaf Mountain and Christ the Redeemer Statue, in Botafogo, 8km from central Rio and close to the beaches. The school's focus is to develop character, spiritual values, social awareness, discover individual talents and develop interpersonal skills so the children learn to become responsible citizens in any culture.

Associacao Escola Graduada de São Paulo – www.graded.br

The school was established in 1920 to educate the children of employees of American companies and the American Chamber of Commerce.

Graded school is a private day school for children between 2–18 years. The school is divided into lower school, for two years to grade 5; middle school consists of grades 6–8 and high school with grades 9–12. Students are prepared for a general American high school diploma with options for a Brazilian high school diploma or an International Baccalaureate Diploma.

Tuition fees are available on request.

Chapel International School-www.chapelschool.com

Chapel School, established 60 years ago, is an American international school in a quiet residential area of São Paulo with 700 students from pre-school to high school. The curriculum is designed for a Brazilian, American and International Baccalaureate.

Tuition fees are available on request.

Pan American Christian Academy, São Paulo – www.paca.com.br

Pan American Christian Academy, São Paulo, states its mission as aiming to develop young people through quality education based on faith. It is accredited by the Brazilian Ministry of Education and Culture as well as the Southern Association of Colleges and Schools. Stretching out over eight acres in Rio Bonito, South São Paulo, it caters for children from the ages of three to 18.

American Schools of Belo Horizonte – www.eabh.com.br

The school is located approximately 15 minutes from downtown. The campus comprises a 10-acre site and offers a pre-preparatory course to high school.

American School of Brasília – www.eabdf.br

The school lies on a five-acre campus in the heart of Brasília and was established in the same year as the city itself. Enrolment averages around 450 children. Approximately 65% of the children are Brazilian, 15% American and the remainder represent nearly 23 different nationalities.

The school is fully accredited by the Southern Association of Colleges and Schools of the United States.

Tuition fees are available on request.

American School of Campinas, São Paulo – www.aassa.com

The American School in Campinas was founded in 1956 by 3M, one of the first American companies in Campinas. It is fully accredited by the Southern Association of Colleges and Schools and is a member of American Schools in South America. It offers pre-school teaching from ages 3–6 and employs the Montessori Method.

American School of Recife, Pernambuco – www.ear.com.br

The school offers enrolment from pre-preparatory to high school, preparing students for university education in Brazil, America and Europe.

Over 80 % of the students at the school are Brazilian, and fewer than 10% are American.

Pan American School of Porto Alegre, Rio Grande do Sul – www.panamerican.com.br

The school moved to a new site in 2007 and enrols children from ages 3–18.

International School of Curitiba – www.isc-cic.com.br

The school provides education from pre-preparatory to high school. It has two campuses located in a residential setting close to downtown Curitiba.

Pan American School of Bahia – www.escolapanamerica.com

The school founded in 1960 is cooperatively owned by the parents and offers a college preparatory institution for American, International and Brazilian children.

The school offers an early childhood programme for 3–4 year olds, an elementary unit for kindergarten; middle school and a four-year high school. A number of high school students participate in an exchange programme with the USA. The school is accredited through the Southern Association of Colleges and Schools in USA.

Chapter 9

Culture and sports

It's widely understood that football plays a major role in everyday life in Brazil. But Brazil is rich in culture, too.

MUSIC AND CARNIVAL

The most recognised aspect of Brazilian culture is a love of music and the celebration that everyone knows as *Carnaval*. This takes place in its own idiosyncratic style all over the country in the month of February and officially lasts four days, during the Brazilian summer holidays.

After 500 years of African and European influence, the world famous carnival music is an eclectic mix – the Brazilian national dance *samba* is played with African drums. Another popular form of music in Brazil is the *bossa nova*, created by Brazilian artists Antonio Carlos Jobim and João Gilberto in the late 1950s and popularised throughout the world by Frank Sinatra and the cover version of the song *Girl from Ipanema* originally sung by João Gilberto's wife, Astrud Gilberto.

Once the carnival fever has expired, there are many other attractions that Brazil can offer the discerning visitor, some of which are mentioned below.

REGIONAL ATTRACTIONS

Things to do and places of interest in the city of Rio de Janeiro

The Brazilian Academy of Letters is a copy of the Petit Trianon of Paris which includes a library with 90,000 books. There are guided tours of the building.

■ Flamengo Embankment is over 1,000,000 square metres of gardens stretching from Santos Dumont airport to the Botafogo Cove offering a number of sporting attractions. It is also called the Brigadeiro Eduardo Gomez Park.

■ Lapa's Arches (Carioca Aqueduct) was built in 1752 to bring water to Rio from the Carioca springs in Santa Teresa. This now acts as a bridge for the Santa Teresa street car.

■ The National Library is the largest library in Latin America (with 15 million books) and of which there are guided tours.

■ One of the most ostentatious buildings in Rio is the Colombo Confectioners' Building which was founded in 1894 – a magnificent *belle époque* building in which to laze away an afternoon in the sumptuous tea rooms.

■ Copacabana Palace Hotel is a Brazilian historical heritage site, dating from 1923, attracting celebrities from every age and sphere.

■ Christ the Redeemer statue, measuring 38 metres in height, sits on top of the Corcovado Hill, which itself measures 710 metres in height. It was opened in 1931 and is known as the wonder of Rio as well as one of the new wonders of the modern world. The Corcovado railway that takes you to the statue dates back to 1884.

■ The Tijuca National Park is 20km from the centre of Rio and is claimed to be the largest urban forest in the world, measuring over 3,300 hectares – ten times larger than New York's Central Park. It includes forests, trails, waterfalls, over 300 species of flora and fauna as well as specimen trees over 100 years old. The landmarks of Pico da Tijuca (1,020 metres), the Pedra da Gavea (842 metres) and the Pedra Bonita (696 metres) can all be found in the park. There are free guided tours every other Sunday.

■ The Copacabana Fortress was built in 1914 as a defensive position. Inside the fortress are collections of arms and historical military objects.

■ The 18th century Nossa Senhora de Candelaria Church is an example of Brazil's grand past with walls of carved marble, cut stone masonry, bronze works and murals. It is well worth a visit.

■ São Francisco Penitencias Church was erected between 1657 and 1772 and is a wonderful example of baroque architecture and art in Brazil.

■ The Botanical Garden has rare flora and is very much a living museum, ranked by UNESCO as one of the most important bio reserves in the world. It includes imperial palm trees dating from 1808 and many other interesting features including a greenhouse with insect-eating plants.

■ The Rodrigo de Freitas Lagoon is situated in the middle of the districts of Lagoa, Ipanema, Leblon, Gavea and Jardim Botanico. Around this lagoon there are parks, sports courts, skating rings, a heliport, food kiosks, live music and exhibitions.

■ The Maracana Soccer Stadium is one of the largest football stadiums in the world and will be staging the 2014 World Cup final. It was built for the 1950 World Cup when it had an audience of 199,000. It was designed to accommodate 166,000!

■ The São Bento Cloister is a world heritage monument ranked by UNESCO. Although plain on the outside, it is engraved in gold on the inside walls, and has many works of art, many dating from the 18th century.

■ The Modern Art Museum dates from 1958 and holds a collection of 4,000 works, and includes an art cinema, library and bookstore.

■ The National History Museum holds 275,000 items and sits on an 18,000 square metre site, occupying three separate buildings. Interestingly, it holds the plumed pen used by Princess Isabel to sign the Aurea Law, abolishing slavery.

■ The International Museum of Naïf Art hosts works by self taught artists, and is one of the largest collections of its type in the world.

■ The National Museum of Beaux Art has a mixture of Brazilian and International fine art.

■ The Catete Palace houses the Republic Museum and was the old republic building until 1960. It has seen all the important events in the country's history including a suicide by one president.

■ Pao de Acucar (Sugar Loaf Mountain) is a world renowned landmark that can be reached by cable car and was opened in 1912. The peak of the mountain rises to over 396 metres above sea level and is at the mouth of Guanabara Bay. There are two theories as to the name, some say its shape resembles a sugar loaf, but it is more likely that the name derives from the Tupi – Guarani language – and a name given to it of Pau-nh-acuqua, meaning high hill.

■ Quinta Boa Vista Park surrounds the former royal residence including gardens with lakes, grottos and nooks. Also within the park are the National Museum and the city zoo, including playgrounds, picnic areas, sports courts and restaurants.

■ The Roberto Burle Marx Cottage was left to the people by its namesake in the town of Guaratiba. It houses a vast collection of plants and artwork. Roberto was an important landscape artist.

■ The Municipal Theatre is in the heart of Cinelandia and is notable for its architectural design and its wonderful interior decor.

Things to do and places of interest in Petrópolis

The history of the city began with Dom Pedro I who fell in love with the perfect climate, pure air, 16°C year-round temperature and the physical beauty of the hills. He bought the Corrego Seco farm in 1830. This was handed down to Dom Pedro II in 1843 at which point it came to be known as Petrópolis. It still has many of the mansions that were once inhabited by the nobility and the Royal Palace of Dom Pedro II, which is now a museum. Several noted writers and painters live in Petrópolis now, as well as Princess Isabel's grandson, Dom Pedro de Orleans e Braganca, who is, at 94, the heir to the throne! The Rio Negro Palace, which once belonged to a nobleman, has also been the summer residence of presidents from time to time.

■ Other notable buildings include the cathedral of São Pedro de Alcantara.

■ The Imperial Museum is a neo classical building built in 1848 with a wonderful garden and priceless exhibits, including Don Pedro II's crown.

■ The Crystal Palace made of metal and glass was made in France and inaugurated in 1884. This was where Princess Isabel signed the liberation of 103 slaves shortly prior to the abolition of slavery with the Golden Law.

■ The Dedo de Deus is worth seeing. Translated into English this means 'God's Finger' and is so called as it resembles a finger made from a rock formation in the Serra dos Orgaos National Park.

■ The National Park covers over 11,000 hectares and houses many plants and birds some of which would otherwise be extinct, such as the hawk headed parrot. It is a tropical paradise for the nature lover, offering rafting on the Paraibuna river, riding, trekking in the Tingua ecological reserve, walking along the Emperor's Path and a walk of over 32km from Petrópolis to Pati do Alferes over Couto Mountain.

■ There is a municipal park for the less energetic, offering bike paths, basketball courts, sand and play areas, as well as places for festivals.

Things to do and places of interest in Bahia State

Until 1763, Salvador was the throne of the Portuguese Imperial Crown and a very important port in the 18th century. Naturally it has a very mixed population and is considered to be the cultural capital of Brazil.

The city of Salvador da Bahia

The main attractions of Salvador are as varied and numerous as its people. There is a great range and standard of accommodation available in the whole of Salvador. The city offers a rich mix of architectural styles which can be accessed on foot and explored by car. Among the architectural attractions are:

■ the Municipal and Se Plazas;

■ the Lacerda Elevator;

■ the Municipal Palace and Chamber;

■ the Rio Branco Palace;

■ the Archbishop's Palace;

■ the Basilica Cathedral;

■ the Voodoo Terreiro de Jesus.

The city is a UNESCO heritage site and has three basic regions: the first is the city square to The Largo de São Francisco; the second, Pelourinho Largo do Carmo; the third, Largo de Santo Antonio Alem do Carmo.

■ The districts of 'Cruzeiro de São Francisco Square Pelourinho' and Carmo Plaza' in the city have many churches and plazas.

■ The Basilica Cathedral is a 17th century building and contains gold, marble and tortoiseshell in mixed Baroque and Rococo styles.

■ The Church of São Francisco has a convent and was constructed a century after the Franciscan Friars arrived in 1587. This is one of the most impressive churches in Brazil, the building of which commenced at the beginning of the 18th century.

■ The Santo Antonio da Barra Fort is a naval fort from 1536 and can be found in the north entrance of All Saints' Bay.

■ The Monte Serrat Fort belongs to the army and was built in 1583.

There are many museums in Salvador:

■ the Carlos Costa Pinto Museum comprises a family's collection of artefacts;

■ the Sacred Art Museum is located at the Santa Teresa Convent and contains sculptures of various materials including precious and semi precious stones;

■ the Bahia Art Museum was founded in 1918 and is in the Cerqueira Lima Mansion. It houses art and artefacts from the 17th to 19th centuries;

■ the Abelardo Rodrigues Museum has works of art from the 16th to 19th centuries in the Ferrao Solarium.

The city of Porto Seguro

In the centre of Porto Seguro Cidade Alta is a national heritage monument as it was one of the first cities to be created in Brazil. At night there are special illuminations in place to enhance the view of the buildings. Some of the main attractions are:

■ the Monte Pascoal – a national park of nearly 15,000 hectares;

■ the 'Recife de Fora sea park' which can be visited by ship;

■ an Indian Reservation – the Jaquereira where existing members of the Pataxo tribe live in a traditional Amerindian way;

■ the Pirata Island Aquarium Complex combines eco-tourism with nightlife. There are various night-time activities, including the Alcohol cat walk, which takes place on Avenida Portugal. Quadrado Square is the main centre of the city and has many of the usual shops.

The city of Maraú

There are many attractive sites in this relatively unexplored district:

■ the Tremembe waterfalls, which are 30 metres wide and five metres tall;

■ the fishing village Taipus de Dentro can be found on Taipu Mirim Island, in Camamu bay, which has a settlement, urban infrastructure, an inn and restaurant;

■ Campinho village has a harbour and a yacht club as well as inns and a restaurant;

119

■ another fishing village on Sampinho Island, offers a fish restaurant serving fresh lobsters, crab and edible goiamun – a three metre sea crustacean native to the state of Bahia;

■ Barra Grande is the largest community on the peninsula and one of the best viewing points is from Mirante do Morro do Taipu at a height of 51 metres;

■ the Lagoa de Cassangi is a large lagoon with excellent bathing;

■ for the adventurous, there is the Barra Grande trail stretching over 40km and the Tralha Pontal trail which is 20km long;

■ there are several beaches, such Praia de Manguerias where the water is calm, warm and clear. Praia dos Tres Coqueros has large waves, coconut trees and holiday houses. Praia do Taipus de Fora has 7km of natural pools and coral reefs.

Things to do and places of interest in the State of Alagoas

Maceió, its capital, has many attractions:

■ Jaragua is a neighbourhood with lots of bars, nightlife, theatres and restaurants;

■ Cruz das Almas was an Indian cemetery and is now simply a beach;

■ Jatiuca is about 4km north of the town centre and is popular with surfers and for body-building competitions. It has many bars and restaurants;

■ Ponta Verde is a peaceful, natural headland covered in coconut trees;

■ Maceió Yacht Club caters for keen sailors;

■ for families there is Pajucara Beach, which is safe for swimming;

■ there are also floating bars on a coral reef where one can enjoy the beautiful scenery, and on dry land one can watch the beautiful sunset from Avenida das Paz;

■ Sobral District, is generally farm land named after Sobral Pinto, who was a local nobleman;

■ Pontal da Barra is an interesting point where the Mandau pond meets the sea. The dance 'Fandango' originates from this area;

■ for the keen shopper, there is a wide variety of places to shop in Centro.

Things to do and places of interest in the State of Ceará
Fortaleza

The state capital is the port of Fortaleza, which began with the Dutch who arrived 300 years ago and constructed a fort. It is rich in interesting architecture.

The old city has been modernised but has kept its historical buildings, such as:

■ the Fort of Nossa Senhora da Assuncao;

■ the Luz Palace, which housed the headquarters of the state government until around 1970;

■ the old customs' house which is now used as a shop;

■ the old public jail, which has been converted to stalls on the ground floor and a museum above;

For the nature lover there are many varieties of birds in this area and the most popular area for bird spotting is the salt marshes.

There are other numerous attractions in the city:

■ the Fortaleza Metropolitan Cathedral, which was built between 1938 and 1978;

■ the cultural centre, which includes a memorial, an art museum, a cinema, theatre, arts' workshop and a planetarium;

■ the São Luiz cinema, which is the biggest cinema in Brazil. It was built using

Carrarra marble and houses crystal chandeliers. It took 18 years to build and seats 1,800 people;

■ José de Alencar, writer and promoter of nationalism, was born in the city and his house remains. In his famous work *O Guarani* he canvassed the use of a national language rather than the widely-spoken Portuguese;

■ the João Philipe train station was built in 1880 and is still in use today;

■ the Mucuripe lighthouse was erected as a tribute to Princess Isabel and now houses the lighthouse museum;

■ there are many museums in the city, including the museum of Image and Sound.

■ the Maracatu Museum tells the story of the Maracatu tribe of Ceará and exhibits their clothing, house objects and musical instruments.

■ the Rosario Church is the oldest in the city, dating from the 18th century, and the Sagrado Coracao de Jesus Church is on a site of a former dune called Alta da Boa Vista;

■ the Mucuripe Port was the old port, replaced in 1860 by the metallic bridge;

■ the Ingleses Bridge was built from 1923 to be used as a port, but instead is used as a viewing platform for watching sunsets;

■ one of the most famous squares in Fortaleza is the tree-lined Cristo Redentor Square, famous for hosting cultural events. Ferreira Square is named after the pharmacist Antonio Rodrigues Ferreira. Martires Square is also one of the main squares and stands as a national heritage site and includes a number of theatres.

The State of Pernambuco
Recife
The capital of Pernambuco, Recife, is sometimes referred to as the Venice of Brazil because it has many canals, bridges and narrow one-way streets. The coastline provides an interesting array of the old and the new, with colonial architecture

mingling with high-rise buildings. The beach of Boa Viagem is one of Brazil's most popular beaches and is surrounded by many fine restaurants, a reflection of its affluence.

Other cities in the State of Pernambuco include Olinda, Ilha de Itamaraca and Porto de Galinhas. These are the subject of massive investment and are busy with tourists.

Porto de Galinhas is regarded as having one of the most beautiful beaches in Brazil, with warm, clear water, coral reefs, mangroves and coconut trees. It also boasts wide and long lengths of sandy coastline.

Ilha de Itamaraca can be found 50km north of Recife. This is not just popular with tourists but also with investors. Nearby, the archipelago of Fernando de Noronha comprises 21 volcanic islets, which attract divers and snorkelers. There are many inns and one hotel in the area. Fernando de Noronha allows a maximum of 420 visitors at any one time and is regarded as a model environmental protection area.

If rich architectural history is what you desire, Olinda, with its restored and preserved 17th century colonial buildings has been declared a UNESCO world heritage site.

The State of Rio Grande do Norte
Natal
In November 2007 the Ponte Newton Navarro bridge, linking the north to the south of Natal, was opened.

One of the traditional and most-visited areas in the capital city of Natal is Ponte Negra. At one end of the beach is Morro do Careca, which is basically an enormous sand dune 100 metres high. There are beaches at Aria Preta, Artistas and Meio, where there are many very popular bars and small hotels.

The other attractions in Natal are:

■ Genipabu is 25km away and there is an array of enormous dunes and lakes.

■ Pirangi do Norte is 30km away. Here, a boat will take you to places where you can snorkel and dive in the sea.

There is a nature trail in the second largest urban park in Brazil (1,200 hectares), where a lot of the Atlantic forest vegetation has been preserved.

Natal has good transport links; there is an international and national airport and very good bus links.

The State of Paraná

By far the most spectacular and memorable attraction is the Iguaçu Falls in the city of Foz do Iguaçu. The man-made wonder – Itaipu – the world's largest hydroelectric dam is another must-see.

LITERATURE

Having exhausted all the sights and sounds of Brazil, there is an array of writers of fiction one could while away the time with on stormy and thundery days or lazing on the beach on sunnier days.

If the Portuguese language has been mastered, there are many popular historical works of fiction and modern literature. Some are also translated into English.

By far the most popular literary figure in Brazilian fiction is Joaquim Maria Machado de Assis (1839–1908), sometimes referred to Brazil's answer to Shakespeare or Dante. His most popular tale, *Dom Casmurro*, has the same themes as Shakespeare's *Othello* – fear, jealousy and adultery.

One of the most popular fiction writers in Brazil of the 20th century was Jorge Amado (1912–2001). His most popular books, *Gabriella, Clove and Cinnamon* and *Dona Flor and Her Two Husbands* depict, in the words of his friend Jean-Paul Sartre, 'the best example of folk novel'. Both of the books have been made into films.

To find out more information on Brazil's history, *Red Gold* by John Hemming and *The Colonial Background of Modern Brazil* by Caio Prado Junior are worth a read.

For the adventurous reader, *Brazilian Adventure* by Peter Fleming (brother of Ian Fleming, writer of the James Bond books) is a humorous read – "São Paulo is like Reading, only much farther away". The book came about as a result of Peter Fleming replying to an advert in *The Times* newspaper seeking like-minded, adventurous persons to travel in search of Colonel Percy Fawcett who had disappeared somewhere in the Amazon jungle in search of an ancient lost city. Percy Fawcett formed the basis of the fictional character Indiana Jones.

Os Sertoes (*Rebellion in the Backland*) is a serious read by Euclides de Cunha. Although chronicling the military insurgence by the Republican army against Bahia's backland, more importantly, the author discusses Brazil's past, and what lies in the future for the republic of Brazil.

Paulo Coelho is a very successful modern author of fiction, although his work is slighted by the serious literati as being self indulgent and light-weight. That being said, his books have been translated into 63 languages, published in 150 countries and more than 85 million copies have been sold worldwide.

SIGN LANGUAGE

It is wise to be aware of the Brazilian sign language. For example, although in most parts of Europe and North America, the 'OK' sign is commonly used to express agreement by forming a circle with the tips of the thumb and index finger pressed together – in Brazil, it is used to express disdain and in some parts of the country could result in a physical confrontation.

■ To express 'OK' this is done simply by holding up the thumb, accompanied by a big smile.

■ To express disagreement, the index finger is wagged back and forth.

■ To express that one has had enough, simply hold the hand horizontally at one end of the forehead and slide to the other side of the head as if wiping the sweat off the brow.

■ To express that not only have you had enough but you want to be rid of the issue vexing you, slap the hands together outwards whilst placing your hands horizontally towards the chest.

■ Placing the fingers in a circle around the eyes means not that you are as wise as an owl, but that you are greedy.

■ Placing the tip of the middle finger next to the corner of the eye means 'I'm on to you'.

■ Prodding the side of the neck with the tips of your fingers suggests that you are expressing an opinion of dishonesty in the person being addressed and sometimes this is accompanied by vocalising '171' or 'um sete um' – being the number of the section of the criminal code dealing with dishonesty.

SPORTS

Brazilians adore all kinds of sport. Brazil hosted the 2007 Pan American Games, winning 52 gold medals, coming third, after Cuba and the USA. It won 157 medals in total, coming second in the overall medal count, above Cuba and second to USA. Brazil was successful in its bid to host the 2014 FIFA World Cup and has hopes of hosting the 2016 Olympic games.

The principal sporting activity in Brazil is football, although surfing, volleyball, canyoning, rafting, diving, tennis and not least, motor racing, are also popular.

Surfing

The best surfing beaches are in the South East of the country, in the city of Saquarema, in the State of Rio de Janeiro, approximately 100km east of the city of Rio de Janeiro. There are international surfing championships that are held in the district of Itauna, in the city of Saquarema, during the months of May to August. The coastline of Santa Catarina also boasts some of the best beaches for surfing and is a popular location for national championships.

Volleyball

Volleyball is very popular not just as a participant sport, but even more so as a spectator sport. The city of Saquarema, in particular the district of Barra Nova, is home to the national volleyball stadium, set in a picturesque landscape with a spectacular backdrop of mountains and crashing, surfing beaches in front. Naturally, with any country with as large a coastline as Brazil, beach volleyball is bound to be a very popular pastime and sport.

Rafting, canyoning and diving

For the brave and adventurous, and the newcomer, there are many waterways and rafting schools dotted mainly around the south eastern states such as São Paulo and Rio de Janeiro. Rafting is particularly popular in the southern states of Paraná, Santa Catarina and Rio Grande do Sul.

Canyoning is not only popular in the south eastern and southern states of Brazil, but is also popular in the states of Bahia and Sergipe.

For the diving enthusiast, it is estimated that there are approximately 11,000 shipwrecks dotted around Brazil's coastline – only 600 have been located to date. A divers' paradise awaits the treasure hunter. Some popular locations are Arraial do Cabo and Angra dos Reis in the state of Rio de Janeiro, although one of the world's most popular is the archipelago of Fernando de Naronha, in the north eastern state of Pernambuco.

Motor racing

Brazil is a world leader in motor racing and has won many Formula One Grand Prix World Championships since the 1970s with stars such as Emerson Fittipaldi, world champion, 1972 and 1974; Nelson Piquet, world champion 1981, 1983 and 1987 and Ayrton Senna, world champion 1988, 1990 and 1991 before his tragic death in 1994. Most recently, Rubens Barrichello who is now a star in his own right even though he was number two to Michael Schumacher, before his retirement in 2005. In July 2007, Nelson Piquet lost his Brazilian civil driving licence because of offences relating to speeding and was ordered to attend driving lessons.

Tennis

Tennis is also a popular sport, popularised by Gustavo Kuerton, who holds 16 international men's singles titles. By far the most successful female Brazilian tennis player was Maria Esther Bueno, who won 19 grand slams, seven women's singles, 11 women's doubles and one mixed doubles between 1958 and 1966.

Football or *futebol*

Football in Brazil is played on the sand, the road, on grass or even clay and is a way of life deeply affecting the national psyche. One cannot hope to be Brazilian without inside knowledge of the subject. Annually, the teams play for the Brazil Cup between the months of April and December; matches taking place almost every weekend. Everyone is glued to the television set, if they are not actually attending a stadium to watch a live match. It is not something to watch alone – friends and families gather together in homes and bars to watch their teams play, and they take to the street when a goal is scored.

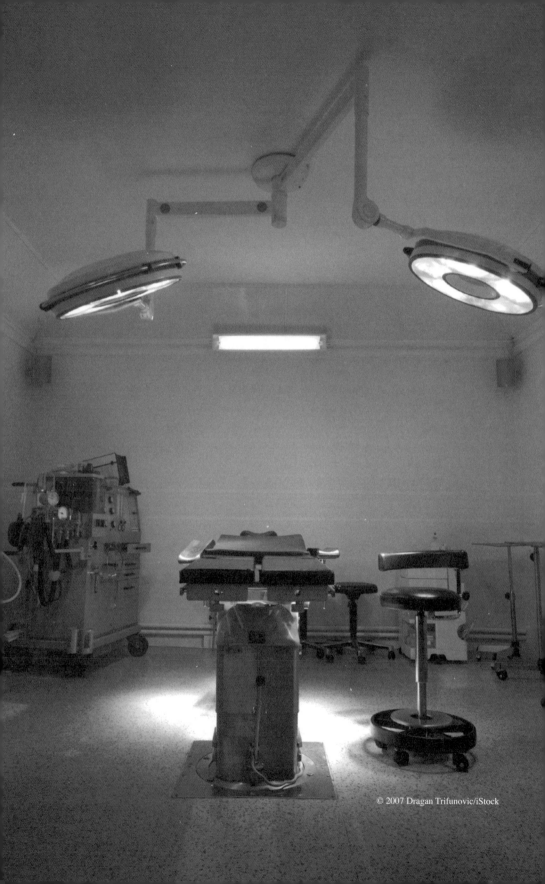

Chapter 10

Cosmetic surgery

It may seem bizarre, but one of the attractions of Brazil is its cosmetic surgeons: this type of tourism is growing and Brazil is there to develop it further.

Brazil is considered one of the top destinations, if not *the* top destination, for non-invasive and invasive cosmetic surgery. It used to rank second behind the USA in terms of actual cosmetic procedures carried out annually. On average, there are around 400,000 procedures carried out in Brazil annually. This is not surprising as there are around 4,000 plastic surgeons in Brazil.

The actual cost of the procedures compared to the UK is about half. For example, the cost of rhinoplasty in a UK private hospital is between £3,000 and £4,000. The same procedure carried out in a UK cosmetic surgery clinic ranges from £3,100 to £3,300, whereas in Brazil the cost is £1,550. Similarly, the cost of a facelift in a UK private hospital varies between £4,300 and £6,000. The cost for the same procedure in a UK cosmetic surgery clinic is between £4,000 and £5,700, whereas in Brazil it costs only £1,948. The cost of surgery on the upper and lower eyelids carried out in a UK private hospital varies between £2,900 and £3,700 and if carried out in a UK cosmetic surgery clinic it varies between £1,950 and £3,700, whereas in Brazil, it costs £1,550. Generally, there is a saving of 50% on the other types of procedures offered by Brazilian companies.

Brazilian plastic surgeons undergo an initial period of six years at medical school, followed by two years in general surgery and then a further period of three years in plastic surgery. It is advisable to check whether the plastic surgeon is a member of the Brazilian Society of Plastic Surgery (SBCP) on the Society's website. The plastic surgeon should also have accreditation from the International Society of Aesthetics and Plastic Surgeons (ISAPS) as well as the American Society for Aesthetics and Plastic Surgery (ASAPS). The medical facilities should be accredited by the Federal and State Medical Councils of Brazil (Conselho Federal de Medicina – CFM and the Conselho Regional de Medicina – CRM).

The procedures are mainly carried out in São Paulo, Rio de Janeiro and Recife, although Fortaleza is fast becoming very popular. Some of the more popular websites include: www.treatmentabroad.net and www.privatehealth.co.uk.

Bahia, 1° Setembro 1948.

Minha querida Mica

Chapter 11

Language

To understand a culture you need to understand its language. To integrate with the locals it is essential to be able to communicate with them — and not just in English.

As already stated, the official language of Brazil is (Brazilian) Portuguese; which is a romance language, deriving largely from Latin roots. Anyone spending a certain amount of time in any country is duty-bound to learn the language of the people. This is especially so in relation to Brazil where foreigners start off on the basis that they are *gringos* and 'not one of us'. Apart from anything else, being able to speak the local language facilitates the ordinary practicalities of everyday living, from ordering food and drinks, reporting a crime to the police, calling an ambulance or the fire brigade to buying things in shops. Many more Brazilians than let on, do understand a certain amount of English; not least because of international communications and forms of entertainment: songs, films and popular culture are driven by forces which communicate in English. As a corollary to the slight national contempt for foreigners, many forms of advertising and signage in shopping malls incorporate English phrases such as 'shopping' 'diner', 'motel' and so forth, in order to suggest sophistication.

Moreover, if you strike deals in Portuguese (even your best attempt at pidgin Portuguese), you stand a far better chance of securing your *a vista* – a 10% discount for ready money – than someone who talks rather loudly and fast in English, French or German. However, you will find that good shops, restaurants and hotels in cities and major tourist areas tend to employ staff who are reasonably proficient in several languages including, French, Spanish and English.

The pronunciation of Brazilian Portuguese sounds, at first, to an English speaker, both sibilant (or lisping) and nasal, and there is a reluctance to attempt it. Moreover, the Rio accent – *carioca* – makes 'r' sound like 'h' – so, for example, in *carioca* pronunciation, 'Rio de Janeiro' is said 'Hio de Janeiho', whereas in Spanish, it is 'Rio de Haneiro'. But, in some parts of Brazil, the 'r' retains a sound more akin to English or English-American. Brazilians tend to pronounce every letter, including vowels at the end of words.

Obviously, a phrase book and a pocket dictionary help enormously. There are many locally-arranged courses in Brazil, as well as individual tuition. CDs, such as those available from Linguaphone are also useful.

ESSENTIAL WORDS AND PHRASES

no	*nao* (*pr.* nowng)
yes	*sim* (*pr.* seeng)
please	*por favor*
thank you	*obrigado* (if you are male) *obrigada* (if you are female)
hello	*ola!* or *oi!* (more akin to 'hi!'), answering the telephone, *pronto* or *pronta* (if female) – i.e. literally 'ready!'
good-bye	*a deus* (*pr.* a dayus) or *tchau, tchau!*
not at all, you're welcome	*de nada*
excuse me	*com licence* (*pr.* kong licengsa)
sorry	*desculpa*
i [don't] understand	*eu [nao] entendo* (*pr.* ee-o [nowng] engtengdo)
just a moment	*um minutinho*
Help!	*Socorro* (*pr.* so-ko-ho)
Where's the loo?	*Onde tem um banheiro?* (*pr.* ong-de teng oom ba-nyay-ro)

How much?	*Quanto?* (*pr.*kwang-to)
How many?	*Quantos?* (m) quantas (f)
please give me ...	*por favor me de ...*
a few	*alguns* (*pr.* ow-goons)
a little	*so um pouquinho* (saw oom pokeenyo)
a lot	*muito* (mweeng-to)
less	*menos* (*pr.* men-os)
many	*muitos* (m) *muitas* (f) (*pr.* mweeng-tos/tas)
more	*mais*
some	*um pouco* (*pr.* oom po-ko)
Do you speak English?	*Voce fala Ingles?* (*pr.* vo-say falla Ingles)
I speak English	*Eu fala Ingles*
Does anyone here speak English?	*Alguem aqui fala Ingles?* (*pr.* ow-geng aa-kee faa-laa eengles?

NUMBERS

one	*um* (*pr.* oom)
two	*dois* (*pr.* doys)
three	*tres* (*pr.* tres)
four	*quarto* (*pr.* kwaa-tro)
five	*cinco* (*pr.* seengko)
six	*seis* (*pr.* says) – note also that in telephone numbers and telling the time, Brazilians use *meia* (*pr.* maya) which means half a dozen, i.e. six
seven	*sete* (*pr.* se-te)
eight	*oito* (*pr.* oy-to)

nine	*nove (pr.* now-ve)
ten	*dez (pr.* dez)
eleven	*onze (pr.* ong-ze)
twelve	*doze (pr.* do-ze)
thirteen	*treze (pr.* tre-ze)
fourteen	*quatorze (pr.* kaa-torr-ze)
fifteen	*quinze (pr.* keeng-ze)
sixteen	*dezeseis (pr.* de-ze-says)
seventeen	*dezeseite (pr.* de-ze-se-te)
eighteen	*dezeoito (pr.* de-zoy-to)
nineteen	*dezenove (pr.* de-ze naw-ve)
twenty	*vinte (pr.* veeng-te)
twenty one	*vinte e um (pr.* veeng-te e oom)
twenty two	*vinte e dois (pr.* veen-te e doys)
thirty	*trinta (pr.* treeng-taa)
forty	*quarenta (pr.* kwaa-reng-taa)
fifty	*cinquenta (pr.* seen-kweng-taa)
sixty	*sessenta (pr.* se-seng-ta)
seventy	*setenta (pr.* se-teng-taa)
eighty	*oitenta (pr.* oy-teng-taa)
ninety	*noventa (pr.* no-veng-taa)
one hundred	*cem* (seng)
one thousand	*mil (pr.* mee-oo)
one million	*um mihao (pr.* oom mee-ly-owng)

Chapter 12

Conclusion

Those who persevere learn to love the rich variety of life Brazil has to offer. It's not always easy, but the effort makes the journey worthwhile.

I am glad that I came to live in Brazil; even though some of the learning curve about how one can expect to be treated has been difficult.

Brazilians are a tough, physically brave, cheerful, friendly, resilient people, with a different attitude towards time and time-keeping than most people in the European and North American world. Although this aspect of their national psyche can, at first, cause frustration with a time-conscious European or North American immigrant or tourist, try to remember that it is probably, at least partly, caused by the weather and the beauty of the country creating a very laid-back approach to life.

The climate is superbly varied from equatorial rainforest, in the north, through tropical and sub-tropical regions, to the temperate regions in the south. This all makes for a wide range of flora and fauna in coastal regions, mountains and plains. In the less tropical areas, the seasons can be quite marked and this means that, overall, virtually anything can be grown in Brazil.

The economy is healthy and word is out that, while the USA and the UK (hard on its heels) are entering recession, Brazil's economy is booming and the exchange rate is swiftly turning in Brazil's favour. Two years ago, there were well over R$2 for US$1; now it is around R$1.57, with rumours that Brazil wants to drive the rate down to parity with the US$. There were, not so long ago, R$5 to GB£1 but now it is closer to R$3.5. This derives from the fact that the Brazilian economy is not closely linked with the economy of the USA or Europe, as well as the fact that Brazil has vast natural resources of oil, wood, metals, gems, and renewable fuels deriving from sugar cane, which the whole world needs.

House prices are generally between one tenth and one twentieth of American and European prices. Houses are solidly built. When you need repairs and you call a tradesman out he will arrive (in due course; although often with a promptness which makes one wonder about other lapses in observances of time-keeping) and make an inspection. If parts are needed for a pump or plumbing, he will give you a choice of materials. By the sea, always opt for plastic as metal corrodes in the salt air. He will go straight away to buy the parts and complete the job; there is seldom any question of waiting a fortnight for parts to arrive.

If your car won't start, call a mechanic (there are plenty to choose from) and he will come to the roadside or your house and either fix the problem or take the car away. All the artisan trades are alive and kicking: metal-workers, carpenters, plumbers, builders, decorators and the suppliers who rely upon them. If you need some bespoke iron railings – they will come and measure, quote, go away and make them and return to fix them. If you want to replace your internal doors with solid Brazilian hardwood doors, they will be made to your requirements very quickly and skilfully and fixed, for the equivalent of about US$100 each: that is bespoke doors, made from wood that is not available anywhere else, for about a twentieth of the cost that it would be in the USA or the UK if the materials were even available there.

If you want fresh fruit, free range eggs, fresh fish and good meat, it is all there; sometimes, the farmers themselves sell it at weekly markets or on roadside barrows. There are no quotas, food mountains, and no waste or shortage and the small farmer will never have heard of GM food production. Needless to say, food often comes in a plain paper bag and there is neither the frustration of battling with excessive cellophane packaging or the waste in its use. Recycling is common – for plastics, glass and paper – and there are many traders who call to ask whether you have any of these things to discard. The rubbish collectors often pass twice a day.

If you need free minor treatment at a health centre it is right there. Often there are free hospitals too.

Communications and means of transport are excellent, both in and out of Brazil with flights to most major cities.

Although I have mentioned the rather troublesome bureaucracy in Brazil, it is true to say that, unless you go out of your way to encounter it, generally speaking there is little day-to-day interference or over-regulation of daily life, as there increasingly is in parts of Europe.

However, be very aware that, as a foreigner, even one with a right of permanent residency, you are, and will be seen as, a guest in Brazil (unless you get to the stage of actually acquiring citizenship, together with perfect Brazilian Portuguese). In Brazil, as in many places, for that matter, some of the locals might harbour resentment towards outsiders coming in and buying property which they could never afford. It is possible to reach an acceptable degree of acceptance and, plainly, any foreigners who give work and spend money in the local community will be received quite well. It also helps to show a cheerful, friendly face, to break any ice.

Do not forget that you need to keep a close eye on deals that you enter into: shop around for everything and do not be shy about asserting your right to the 10% *a vista* – discount for ready cash. Be especially aware that, if a Brazilian introduces you to a shop or a tradesman, he will probably be getting a 10% commission, which will be added to your bill (it seldom comes out of the trader's profit). This is all seen as perfectly normal and if you really let your guard down and allow a builder to buy materials, there is a good chance that, if you do not keep your finger on the pulse and monitor costs, in comparison with other shops, he will have your *a vista* and the commission: so you could end up paying 20% over the odds. And the builder (if he is especially cheeky) might also charge you for his petrol to bring the over-priced goods to your house! Don't show tool sheds stocked with power tools to workmen – who sometimes don't even have their own hand tools. If you get into an argument over an employee, find someone – an educated Brazilian friend – to help, because Brazilian employment rights are, as already described, quite strong enough, without the exaggerations in the figure work that can creep into dismissal claim forms.

After a while, you will find that you get to know the good local tradesmen who do not try to take advantage, especially when they know that you are educated in the local ways and prices. Then, of course, you do not need to rely on introductions from anyone else.

Also remember that Brazilian bureaucracy can involve much technicality and long waiting periods and, during periods of national holiday, such as *Carnaval*, the religious festivals, Republic Day and Independence Day, nothing gets done. Be careful that you are properly advised in relation to all the formal applications which you make; make sure that you file your tax returns if you become a permanent resident, and make sure that the annual local taxes on your house are paid (the *prefeitura* do not always send a bill). If you don't pay an electricity bill on time, you might get one reminder at most and then they just come and cut you off at the electricity pole in the street.

Keep your gates, house and car locked, because opportunistic theft there is, outside the big cities, far more frequent than actual robbery. Wherever you are, don't overdress or wear too much jewellery – and keep away from obviously dangerous areas such as *favellas*.

I have spoken to many well-travelled people who have come to live in Brazil and we all agree on one thing: the pluses very easily out-weigh the minuses. We all favour it as a place to live above anywhere else, especially when we recall, in our fresh ocean or mountain air, previously standing in the crush of a subway train on a grey, Monday morning.

Index